Praise for *Why We Love Dogs,*
Eat Pigs, and Wear Cows

"Melanie Joy's book is an important and groundbreaking contribution to the struggle for the welfare of animals. It helps us step outside the box of 'carnism' so that we are better positioned to think critically and be a part of the solution, helping to create a more compassionate and sustainable world."

—Yuval Harari, *New York Times* bestselling author
of *Sapiens: A Brief History of Humankind*

"An absorbing examination of why humans feel affection and compassion for certain animals but are callous to the suffering of others."

—*Publishers Weekly*

"There's plenty of information in this book, and insight and argument. But the true achievement of *Why We Love Dogs, Eat Pigs, and Wear Cows* is that it reminds us of what we already know. With eloquence and humility, Melanie Joy appeals to the values that all of us already have and have always had. She reminds us of who we are."

—Jonathan Safran Foer, award-winning author of
Everything Is Illuminated, Eating Animals, and *We Are the Weather*

"This is a must-read book for everyone who is horrified by the idea of eating dogs but eats pigs, cows, and chickens. Melanie Joy examines the psychological props that make it possible for us to adore some animals and eat others—and kicks them all aside. *Why We Love Dogs* is written in a clear and lively style, and I'm delighted to see it out in a new edition with a foreword by Yuval Harari."

—Peter Singer, professor of bioethics at Princeton
University, author of *Animal Liberation*

"Melanie Joy is a thought leader whose work is potentially world changing. A few years from now, 'carnism' will be a household term, and how we think about eating animals will be fundamentally altered."

—Maneka Sanjay Gandhi, India's longest-serving member of
Parliament and chairperson of People for Animals, India

"Few books have done more to change the way I think than *Why We Love Dogs, Eat Pigs, and Wear Cows*. This is a framework for thinking about how dominant ideologies disguise, protect, and conserve themselves. It will help you see not just t͟ tionship with animals, but the pre remain hidden all over modern soci

—Ezra Klein, co

"Melanie Joy is one of the great thinkers of our time. Her excellent *Why We Love Dogs, Eat Pigs, and Wear Cows* . . . makes a powerful, novel argument for eating plant-based. Her reasoning transcends just health and is a must-read for anyone who wants to make thoughtful food choices."

—Dan Buettner, National Geographic Fellow and *New York Times* bestselling author of *The Blue Zones*

"*Why We Love Dogs, Eat Pigs, and Wear Cows* is groundbreaking. Melanie Joy brilliantly explains why people resist information that would help them make more healthful food choices—and how they can overcome this."

—Michael Greger, MD, *New York Times* bestselling author of *How Not to Die* and founder of *nutritionfacts.org*

"Why read Melanie Joy? Because her concept of carnism makes us see things differently. Because she addresses readers with empathy. And because she belongs to a new and exciting generation of committed intellectuals. All of these reasons are good. But there is another one that surpasses them all. You have to read Melanie Joy because what she tells us is important."

—Matthieu Ricard, Buddhist monk, photographer, author, and humanitarian

"Melanie Joy's work took me from getting it to living it—all in the time it took me to finish her groundbreaking book."

—Josh Tetrick, founder and CEO, Just

"Melanie Joy is a seer: she sees how and why we humans do what we do and she provides passage through our unconscious behavior so that we can make more thoughtful choices. She is infinitely respectful of the reader, and so we walk away feeling wiser and empowered to be changemakers."

—Kathy Freston, *New York Times* bestselling author of *Quantum Wellness, Veganist,* and *The Lean*

"*Why We Love Dogs* helped me understand the issue of eating animals from a new, unique, and empowering perspective. I highly recommend this book for anyone who wants to make more compassionate, rational, and healthful food choices."

—Daniel Negreanu, six-time World Series of Poker bracelet winner and member of the Poker Hall of Fame

WHY WE
LOVE DOGS
EAT PIGS
AND
WEAR COWS

AN INTRODUCTION TO CARNISM

Melanie Joy, PhD

Foreword by Yuval Noah Harari

Red Wheel

This edition first published in 2020 by Red Wheel, an imprint of
Red Wheel/Weiser, LLC
With offices at:
65 Parker Street, Suite 7
Newburyport, MA 01950
www.redwheelweiser.com

ISBN: 978-1-59003-501-6

Library of Congress Cataloging-in-Publication Data available upon request

Cover design by Kathryn Sky-Peck
Interior by Steve Amarillo / Urban Design LLC
Typeset in Baskerville and PMN Caecilia

Printed in the United States of America
IBI
10 9   8 7 6 5 4 3 2 1

For witnesses everywhere.
Through your eyes, we may find our way.

The greatness of a nation and its moral progress can be judged by the way its animals are treated.

—MAHATMA GANDHI

CONTENTS

ACKNOWLEDGMENTS

This book is the result of a project that began many years ago, with an idea that turned into a doctoral dissertation, which then grew into the volume it is today. Over the years, many people helped shape my ideas and hone my words, and supported me as a professional and a person. To them I am eternally grateful. I want to thank Aimee Houser, my brilliant and inspiring editor, who worked with me every step of the way; my agent, Patti Breitman, who believed in my work and made sure it found a home; Clare Seletsky, who carried this project through the home stretch; Caroline Pincus and Bonni Hamilton of Red Wheel/Weiser, for their enthusiasm and support; Carolyn Zaikowski, who insisted that I write this book; Bonnie Tardella, for her tireless editing; Janice Goldman, George Bournakis, Herb Pearce, and Susan Solomon for being my lifelines; Anna Meigs, for her wisdom and guidance; Ruth and Jake Tedaldi, for helping me when I most needed it; Teri Jessen, for her vision; Bonnie and Perry Norton, for believing in me and giving me the opportunity to carry out my work; Fred and Claudette Williams; Dina Aronson; John Adams; Stephen Cina; Adam Wake; Linda Riebel; Michael Greger; Zoe Weil; V. K. Kool; Ken Shapiro; Stephen Shainbart; Hillary Rettig; Rita Agrawal; Eric Prescott; Laureano Batista; Josh Balk; and Robin Stone. I also want to thank my friends and family who have supported me throughout a very long journey. Finally, I want to thank Josh Balk; Stacey Wells; Daniel Braune; Theresa Lukassowitz; Cristina Castellan; Michelle Schaefer; Sana Al-Badri; my brilliant and beloved husband, Sebastian Joy;

and my team at Beyond Carnism, for their invaluable support for the new edition; and I thank Yuval Harari, for the compelling and insightful new foreword he provided and for the invaluable work he is doing in the world.

FOREWORD TO THE TENTH ANNIVERSARY EDITION

If an Olympic-style competition were taking place to determine who was the most miserable creature on Earth today, it is likely that the gold medal candidates competing head to head would be the cows, chickens, and pigs we raise to satisfy our whims and needs. Why do these animals have such horrible lives?

It may seem like domesticated animals have a good life, especially compared to wild animals. Think of a cow on a dairy farm and a zebra on the African savanna for example. The zebra spends her entire day searching for food and water, which she doesn't always find. The zebra is constantly threatened by predators, diseases, and natural disasters like floods and droughts. Domesticated cows, in contrast, seem to enjoy the constant care of the farmers who supply them with food, water, vaccines, and medications, and protect them against predators and natural disasters. However, despite what many of us have learned to believe, farm animals live in conditions that we'd probably find reprehensible were they the conditions that dogs or cats lived in—and these individuals nevertheless sooner or later find themselves in the slaughterhouse. Even in instances where farm animals' basic physical needs *are* met, their social and emotional needs are ignored. Modern agriculture treats these animals as machines for the production of milk, meat, and eggs, and not as creatures with a rich world of feelings and sensations.

To understand the emotional world of farm animals, we need to look not merely at their living conditions in twenty-first-century industrialized society, but to those of their ancestors thousands and millions of years ago. Examining historical roots in order to understand modern experience is the province of the scientific field of evolutionary psychology, and its findings are relevant for all animals—for cows, chickens, and humans, too. Consider, for example, our passion for sweet and fatty foods. In the twenty-first century, there is no sense to this passion. In fact, it is destructive. Today, on Earth, many more people die of obesity and diabetes than from hunger, wars, and terrorism combined. The average person has a much greater chance of dying from overeating at McDonald's than from an Al-Qaeda attack. So why do we do this to ourselves?

Because our world of feelings and sensations evolved to help us thrive not in today's industrial society, but in the world of our ancestors, tens of thousands of years ago in the African savanna. Fifty thousand years ago, an ancestor of mine was walking through the African savanna and ran into a tree full of ripe, sweet fruit. The right reaction in this situation was to eat as much fruit as possible, as soon as possible, before the baboons from the neighboring troop would eat them all. If my ancestor had a rare genetic mutation that would have made her dislike sweet and fatty foods, she probably would not have survived. When I open the refrigerator door in my house today and see chocolate cake, the DNA and the neurons in my brain do not realize that I live in the twenty-first century; they still think I am in the African savanna, hence, I will feel a strong urge to eat the cake.

The same applies to other animals as well. Consider, for example, the need for puppies to play. Why do they like to play so much? Because tens of thousands of years ago, a game was necessary for the vital survival of their ancestors, the wolves. Wolves are social animals. They cannot survive and reproduce unless they cooperate with other wolves. The way wolves learn the rules of the game in their society is largely by playing games. A wolf puppy who did not feel a strong urge to play due to a rare genetic mutation would not survive.

What happens if today we take a small puppy, isolate him in a cage, give him water, food, and medicine, and when he reaches puberty, take his sperm and inseminate a female dog in heat? This puppy no longer needs to play to survive. But he will still feel a strong urge to play, which is why if we keep him locked in a cage his whole life, he will be very miserable, despite receiving food and shelter. This is because his emotional needs do not reflect his present state, but rather the influence of earlier evolutionary processes.

This is also true for farm animals, of course. Even if farmers provide their cows and chickens with sufficient food, water, medicine, and shelter, they ignore their emotional and social needs, and these animals experience intense suffering.

We can, of course, pose the difficult question of whether it is right to attribute emotions and social needs to animals. Aren't we guilty of humanizing animals, like a little boy who runs into a table and imagines the table hurt him intentionally, having feelings and intentions as if it were a human being? Well, to the best of scientists' understanding, this is by no means humanizing. Emotions are not some spiritual trait that God has given only to humans so they can write poetry and enjoy music. Emotions are biochemical mechanisms that have evolved through natural selection processes, to allow animals to solve the problems they encounter every day, so they can survive and multiply. To the best of our knowledge, all mammals and birds and at least some reptiles and fish have feelings. Therefore, when I say the cow has feelings, I do not view the cow as a human being. I view her as a mammal. And that's fine, because indeed, she is a mammal.

What does it mean that emotions are biochemical mechanisms for problem-solving? Consider the following problem, for example: a baboon sees a bunch of bananas hanging on a tree, but notices a lion not far from the tree. Should the monkey try to get the bananas, and risk being devoured by the lion? Basically, this is a mathematical problem of calculating probabilities. Is the probability that the monkey will starve if he does not eat those bananas greater than the probability that he will be devoured by the lion if he tried to get them?

To solve the problem, the monkey has to take many variables into account: What is the distance between me and the bananas? How far is the lion from the bananas? What is my maximum running speed? What is the lion's running speed? Is the lion full and sleepy, or is he hungry and alert? And what about the bananas? Three small, green bananas are a completely different story from ten big, ripe bananas. But these external variables are not sufficient. To make a truly wise decision, the monkey must also take his internal state into account. What is the level of energy in his body? If he has very little energy, he may starve to death, so it is worth taking a risk, even a high one, for the bananas. If the monkey has a lot of energy at the moment and the bananas are nothing more than a luxury, it's not worth taking the risk.

All these variables should be calculated. If the calculation is accurate, the monkey will survive and pass his genes on. An overly cowardly monkey—one who attributes too much severity to danger—will starve to death, and the genes that shaped this cowardly monkey will not be passed onto the next generation. A reckless monkey—one who does not attach sufficient importance to danger—will be eaten by the lion, and the reckless genes will not be passed on to the next generation. Evolution is based on statistics, which filter the various species every minute of every day, and the next generation receives the genes of the animals whose calculations have optimally calculated the data.

But how exactly does the calculation process take place? The monkey does not pull a pencil out from behind his ear, a notebook from the inside pocket of his suit, and start calculating running speeds and energy levels. The monkey also does not have a calculator. The monkey's body and feelings are the calculator. What we refer to in our everyday language as emotions, feelings, and sensations are actually calculations. The monkey feels hungry or full, he senses the lion as more or less threatening, he feels temptation or repulsion for the bananas. In a fraction of a second, the monkey will experience a rush of sensations, feelings, and desires, which is the process of the calculation; and the result of the process will also be expressed as a feeling: the monkey will suddenly be filled with lust and courage, his chest will swell, he will breathe deeply, all his muscles will stretch out and then . . . Go! To the bananas! Or he will be filled with fear, his shoulders will be bent, and all his muscles will relax. Oh, Mama! There's a lion here! Help! And sometimes the numbers balance so well that it is difficult to reach a decision, and the monkey will be filled with confusion and hesitation. Yes . . . no . . . Should I . . . Should I not . . . Damn it! I don't know what to do!

Obviously, there are differences between the feelings of different animals, such as monkeys and cows, and between the feelings of human beings. There are unique emotions that are characteristic of humans only. Shame, for example, is probably such an emotion. Cows do not (to our knowledge) feel shame. There are probably also unique feelings for other animals, which we do not know of, of course.

But there are basic emotions common to all mammals. Perhaps the most basic emotion that defines mammals is the love between a mother and her offspring. Indeed, this emotion gives mammals their name. The word "mammal" comes from the Latin *mamma*, meaning breast. The emotional system that defines me and you as mammals is one where mothers love their offspring so much that they allow them to suckle from their body, and the youngsters, on their side, feel an overwhelming desire to bond with their mothers and stay near them. A baby mammal who for some reason was born indifferent to his mother would not survive for long. A mammalian mother who was born indifferent to her offspring due to a rare mutation may live a long and comfortable life, but her genes will not pass on to future generations. This system works the same way with cows, dogs, whales, and hedgehogs. And since little mammals cannot survive without close maternal help, other emotions can be debated; but it is clear that maternal love and a strong bond between a mother and her offspring characterize all mammals.

It took scientists many years to recognize this. Until recently, psychologists questioned the existence and importance of the emotional bond between mother and offspring even in humans. In the first half of the twentieth century, psychology was dominated by the behaviorist approach, which argued that the relationship between parents and children was based on material feedback: that all that children need is food, medicine, and shelter; and that children are attached to their parents only because they provide for their material needs. Children who also demanded warmth, hugs, and kisses were considered "spoiled," and childcare experts warned parents that if they embraced and kissed their children, the children would grow up to be dependent and egotistical and lack self-confidence.

John Watson, one of the best-known experts in childhood at the time, recommended to parents in 1928, "Never hug or kiss your children and never let them sit on you; if you must, kiss them once on the forehead when you say good night. In the morning, settle for a handshake." The magazine *Infant Care*, popular among American parents in the 1920s and 1930s, explained to parents that the right principles for raising children were to maintain discipline and satisfy their material needs on a regular schedule. In a 1929 issue, parents were told that when a toddler cries because he is hungry when it is time for food, "do not hold him, do not swing him so he will stop crying, and don't feed him unless it is the exact time of eating. It will not hurt the baby to cry, even a newborn baby."

One of the people who ended up challenging this approach was the American psychologist Harry Harlow, who specialized in primate research. In the 1950s and 1960s, Harlow conducted a series of experiments on Rhesus monkeys. He separated small monkeys from their mothers immediately after birth, and raised them in isolated cages. Harlow put a mother monkey doll into each cage. One "mother" was a doll made of metal wires. It was equipped with a bottle of milk that the monkey could suck. A second "mother" was made of wood with a coating of cloth and velvet to give her the same feeling as a real monkey, but she did not have a bottle. In keeping with the basic assumptions of behavioral psychology, Harlow guessed that the little monkeys would cling to a metal mother who supplied their material needs and would not be interested in the useless velvet mother.

To Harlow's surprise, the monkeys clung to the velvet mother and preferred to spend almost all their time with her. From time to time, they went to the metal mother to nurse milk, but then they returned immediately to the arms of the velvet mother. Harlow guessed that the monkeys were cold and that they had clung to the velvet mother to warm up. He installed a white light bulb inside the metal mother, so that she would emit more warmth than the velvet. It did not help. Most of the monkeys continued to favor the velvet mother so much so that when the two mothers were placed close together, the monkeys continued to hang on to the velvet mother even when they were suckling from the metal mother's milk bottle.

Harlow concluded that the monkeys were looking to the velvet mother for something beyond nutrition and body heat. They were looking for an emotional bond. Millions of years of evolution had imprinted a strong need for emotional attachment in the baby monkeys, as well as the assumption that there is a better chance of developing an emotional bond with soft and furry things than hard and metallic things. This is why small children develop emotional bonds with dolls, blankets, and rags, and not with wooden blocks, stones, and forks. For those baby monkeys, the need for an emotional bond was so great that they abandoned the feeding iron doll and turned their attention to the only object in the environment that seemed to be able to satisfy this need. Unfortunately, the velvet mother did not really create an emotional bond with them. Therefore, even though all their material needs were provided, the monkeys grew up with many psychological complexes and, in adulthood, failed to integrate into monkey society and produce their own offspring.

Harlow's research—though cruel to the monkeys—helped revolutionize the understanding of human emotional bonding. Today it is clear to every reasonable person that children, from their very first day, have emotional needs, and that their mental and physical health depends on satisfying these needs no less than the supply of food, medicines, and shelter. This is of course true not only for human children, but also for the offspring of other mammals. After all, Harlow's research was not conducted on sapiens.

Like the experts on childrearing a century ago, farmers throughout history also focused on the material needs of calves, lambs, and foals, and tended to ignore their emotional needs (except in cases where this emotional need served the interests of humans). Thus, for example, the dairy industry, since the agricultural revolution and to the present day, is based on breaking the most basic emotional bond in the mammalian world and separating the offspring from the mother. A cow will not give milk unless she has given birth to a calf, and therefore dairy farmers make sure the cows will give birth to more and more calves. But the calves are separated from their mothers shortly after they are born, and they pass their childhood without the touch of their mother's tongue, her nipples, or her body. What Harry Harlow did on a small scale—to a few hundred rhesus mother monkeys and baby monkeys—the dairy industry is doing to hundreds of millions of individuals.

Today, more than 90 percent of the world's large animals are farm animals: cows, pigs, sheep, and chickens. Billions of animals with a rich world of feelings, emotions, sensations, needs, and fears pass their lives as machines for producing meat, milk, and eggs in industrial production lines. It is the responsibility of each and every one of us to be aware of the immense suffering that we humans are causing these animals and to do our best to reduce this suffering.

Melanie Joy's book is an important and groundbreaking contribution to the struggle for the welfare of animals. It explains eloquently how the global system of animal exploitation has been created, what keeps it going, and how it puts an unbearable burden on billions of creatures while most of us fail to pay attention or feel any need to change the situation. This book helps us step outside the box of "carnism" so that we are better positioned to think critically and be a part of the solution, helping to create a more compassionate and sustainable world.

—Yuval Noah Harari, author of
Sapiens: A Brief History of Humankind

CHAPTER 1

To Love or To Eat?

We don't see things as they are; we see them as we are.
—ANAIS NIN

Imagine, for a moment, the following scenario: You are a guest at an elegant dinner party. You're seated with the other guests at an ornately set table. The room is warm, candle-light flickers across crystal wineglasses, and the conversation is flowing freely. Mouthwatering smells of rich foods emanate from the kitchen. You haven't eaten all day, and your stomach is growling.

At last, after what feels like hours, your friend who is host-ing the party emerges from the kitchen with a steaming pot of savory stew. The aromas of meat, seasonings, and vegetables fill the room. You serve yourself a generous portion, and after eating several mouthfuls of tender meat, you ask your friend for the recipe.

"I'd be happy to tell you," she replies. "You begin with five pounds of golden retriever meat, well marinated, and then . . ." *Golden retriever?* You probably freeze midbite as you consider her words: the meat in your mouth is from a *dog.*

What now? Do you continue eating? Or are you revolted by the fact that there's golden retriever on your plate, and you've just eaten some? Do you pick out the meat and eat the vegetables around it? If you are like most people (particularly in the Western world), when you hear that you've been eating dog, your feelings would automatically change from pleasure to some degree of revulsion.* You might also become turned off by the vegetables in the stew, as if they were somehow tainted by the meat.

But let's suppose that your friend laughs and says she was playing a practical joke. The meat isn't golden retriever, after all, but beef. How do you feel about your food now? Is your appetite fully restored? Do you resume eating with the same enthusiasm you had when you first began your meal? Chances are, even though you know that the stew on your plate is exactly the same food you were savoring just moments earlier, you would have some residual emotional discomfort, discomfort that might continue to affect you the next time you sit down to beef stew.

What's going on here? Why is it that certain foods cause such emotional reactions? How can a food, given one label, be considered highly palatable and that same food, given another, become virtually inedible? The stew's main ingredient—meat—didn't really change at all. It was animal flesh to begin with, and it remained that way. It just became— or seemed to, for a moment—meat from a different animal. Why is it that we have such radically different reactions to beef and dog meat?

The answer to these questions can be summed up by a single word: *perception*. We react differently to different types of meat not because there is a physical difference between them, but because our perception of them is different.

THE PROBLEM WITH EATING DOGS

Such a shift in perception can feel like a shift in lanes on a two-lane road: crossing the yellow line radically alters our experience. The reason we can have such a powerful response

---

* Although some individuals might be intrigued rather than repulsed at the idea of eating dogs, in much of the world these people represent a minority. This scenario describes the general experience of people from cultures where eating dogs is not a social norm.

to a shift in perception is because our perceptions determine, in large part, our reality; how we perceive a situation—the meaning we make of it—determines what we think and how we feel about it. In turn, our thoughts and feelings often determine how we will act. Most people perceive dog meat very differently than they do beef; therefore, dog meat evokes very different mental, emotional, and behavioral responses.*

One reason we have such different perceptions of beef and dog meat is because we view cows** and dogs very differently. The most frequent—and often the only—contact we have with cows is when we eat (or wear) them. But for a large number of people, our relationship with dogs is, in many ways, not terribly different from our relationship with people: We call them by their names. We say goodbye when we leave and greet them when we return. We share our beds with them. We play with them. We buy them gifts. We carry their pictures in our wallets. We take them to the doctor when they're sick and may spend thousands of dollars on their treatment. We bury them when they pass away. They make us laugh; they make us cry. They are our helpers, our friends, our family. We love them. We love dogs and eat cows not because dogs and cows are fundamentally different—cows, like dogs, have feelings, preferences, and consciousness—but because our *perception* of them is different. And, consequently, our perception of their meat is different as well.

---

* In cultures around the world, it is common to reject the meat of certain animal species. And taboos regarding the consumption of meat are far more common than those regarding any other foods.[1] Moreover, violations of meat taboos cause the strongest emotional reactions—generally, disgust—and are accompanied by the most severe sanctions.[2] Consider the dietary prohibitions put forth by the major religions of the world; whether the restriction is temporary (as when Christians avoid meat during Lent) or permanent (as with some Buddhists who maintain a vegetarian lifestyle), meat is almost always the object of the taboo.

** Though beef comes from both cows and steers, for simplicity and style I use "cows" throughout this chapter to refer to all bovines.

Not only do our perceptions of meat vary based on the species of animal it came from, but different humans may also perceive the same meat differently. For example, a Hindu might have the same response to beef as an American Christian would to dog meat. These variations in our perceptions are due to our *schema*. A schema is a psychological framework that shapes—and is shaped by—our beliefs, ideas, perceptions, and experiences, and it automatically organizes and interprets incoming information. For example, when you hear the word "nurse," you probably envision a woman who wears a medical uniform and works in a hospital. Even though a number of nurses are male, dress nontraditionally, or work outside of a hospital, unless you are frequently exposed to nurses in a variety of settings, your schema will maintain this generalized image. Generalizations are the result of schemas doing what they're supposed to: sorting through and interpreting the vast amount of stimuli we're constantly exposed to and then putting it into general categories. Schemas act as mental classification systems.

We have a schema for every subject, including animals. An animal can be classified, for instance, as prey, predator, pest, pet, or food. How we classify an animal, in turn, determines how we relate to them—whether we hunt them, flee from them, exterminate them, love them, or eat them. Some overlap can occur between categories (an animal can be prey *and* food), but when it comes to meat—or eggs or dairy products*—most animals are either food, or not food. In other words, we have a schema that classifies animals as edible or inedible.**

---

* Consider, for instance, how most Westerners wouldn't eat crows' eggs or drink cats' milk.

** Schemas can be hierarchically structured, with subschemas embedded in more complex or general schemas. For example, we have a general schema for "animal" and within this are sub-schemas of "edible" and "inedible." These subschemas, in turn, can be broken down into further subschemas; for instance "edible" animals may consist of "wild game," and "domesticated" or "farmed" animals.

And something interesting happens when we are confronted with the meat, eggs, or dairy from an animal we've classified as inedible: we automatically picture the living animal from whom it came, and we tend to feel disgusted at the notion of eating it. The perceptual process follows this sequence:

golden retriever meat (stimulus) ⟶ inedible animal (belief/ perception) ⟶ image of living dog (thought) ⟶ disgust (feeling) ⟶ refusal or reluctance to eat (action)

Let's go back to our imagined dinner party, when you were told you were eating golden retriever. Had such a situation actually occurred, you would have smelled the same smells and tasted the same flavors as you had just moments before. But now your mind probably would have formed a picture of a golden retriever, perhaps bounding across a yard chasing a ball, curled up next to a fire, or running alongside a jogger. And with these images would likely come emotions such as empathy or concern for the dog who had been killed and thus disgust at the thought of eating that animal.

In contrast, if you are like most people, when you sit down to eat beef you don't envision the animal from whom the meat was derived. Instead, you simply see "food," and you focus on its flavor, aroma, and texture. When confronted with beef, we generally skip the part of the perceptual process that makes the mental connection between meat and the living animal. Sure, we all know that beef comes from an animal, but when we eat it, we tend to avoid thinking about this fact. Literally thousands of people with whom I have spoken, both through my professional work and personally, have admitted that if they actually thought about a living cow while eating beef they would feel uneasy—and sometimes even unable to eat it. This is why many people avoid eating meat that resembles the animal from whom it was procured; rarely is our meat served with the head or other body parts intact. In one interesting study, for instance, Danish researchers found that people were uncomfortable eating meat that resembled its animal source, preferring to eat minced meat rather than whole cuts of meat.[3] Yet even if we do make the conscious connection between beef and cows, we still feel less disturbed eating beef than we would eating golden retriever, since (in many cultures) dogs are not meant to be eaten.

How we feel about an animal and how we treat them, it turns out, has much less to do with what kind of animal they are than about what our perception of them is. We believe it's appropriate to eat cows but not dogs, so we perceive cows as edible and dogs as inedible and act accordingly. And this process is cyclical; not only do our beliefs ultimately lead to our actions, but our actions also reinforce our beliefs. The more we don't eat dogs and do eat cows, the more we reinforce the belief that dogs are inedible and cows are edible.

ACQUIRED TASTE

While human beings may have an innate tendency to favor sweet flavors (sugar having been a useful source of calories) and to avoid those that are bitter and sour (such flavors often indicate a poisonous substance), most of our taste is, in fact, made up. In other words, within the broad repertoire of the human palate, we like the foods we've learned we're supposed to like. Food, particularly food from animals, is highly symbolic, and it is this symbolism, coupled with and reinforced by tradition, that is largely responsible for our food preferences. For example, few people enjoy eating caviar until they're old enough to realize that liking caviar means they're sophisticated and refined; and in China, people eat animals' penises because they believe these organs affect sexual function.

Despite the fact that taste is largely acquired through culture, people around the world tend to view their preferences as rational and any deviation as offensive and disgusting. For instance, many people are disgusted at the thought of drinking milk that's been extracted from cows' udders. Others cannot fathom eating bacon, ham, beef, or chicken. Some view the consumption of eggs as akin to the consumption of fetuses (which, in some ways, it is). And consider how you might feel at the notion of eating deep-fried tarantula (hair, fangs, and all), as they do in Cambodia; sour, pickled ram's testicle pâté, as some do in Iceland; or duck embryos—eggs that have been fertilized and contain partially formed birds with feathers, bones, and incipient wings—as they do in some parts of Asia. When it comes to animal foods, all taste may be acquired taste.[4]

THE MISSING LINK

It is an odd phenomenon, the way we react to the idea of eating dogs and other inedible animals. Even stranger, though, is the way we *don't* react to the idea of eating cows and other edible animals. There is an unexplained gap, a missing link, in our perceptual process when it comes to edible species; we fail to make the connection between meat* and its animal source. Have you ever wondered why, out of tens of thousands of animal species, you probably feel disgusted at the idea of eating all but a tiny handful of them? What is most striking about our selection of edible and inedible animals is

---

* Although people tend to be less uncomfortable connecting eggs and dairy products with their animal source, they likely *would* be disgusted were the source of such products an inedible animal, such as a canary or an elephant. They would probably also be disgusted were they to witness the production of eggs or dairy up close.

not the *presence* of disgust, but the *absence* of it. Why are we *not* averse to eating the very small selection of animals we have deemed edible?[5]

The evidence strongly suggests that our lack of disgust is largely, if not entirely, learned. We aren't born with our schemas; they are constructed. Our schemas have evolved out of a highly structured belief system. This system dictates which animals are edible, and it enables us to consume them by protecting us from feeling any emotional or psychological discomfort when doing so. The system teaches us how to *not feel*. The most obvious feeling we lose is disgust, yet beneath our disgust lies an emotion much more integral to our sense of self: our empathy.

FROM EMPATHY TO APATHY

But why must the system go to such lengths to block our empathy? Why all the psychological acrobatics? The answer is simple: because we care about animals, and we don't want them to suffer. And because we eat them. Our values and behaviors are incongruent, and this incongruence causes us a certain degree of moral discomfort. In order to alleviate this discomfort, we have three choices: we can change our values to match our behaviors, we can change our behaviors to match our values, or we can change our *perception* of our behaviors so that they *appear* to match our values. It is around this third option that our schema of meat, eggs, and dairy is shaped. As long as we neither value unnecessary animal suffering nor stop eating animals, our schema will distort our perceptions of animals and the foods procured from their bodies, so that we can feel comfortable enough to consume them. And the system that constructs our schema equips us with the means by which to do this.

The primary tool of the system is *psychic numbing*. Psychic numbing is a psychological process by which we disconnect, mentally and emotionally, from our experience; we "numb" ourselves. In and of itself, psychic numbing is not evil; it is a normal, inevitable part of daily life, enabling us to function in a violent and unpredictable world and to cope with our pain if we do fall prey to violence. For instance, you would likely be hard-pressed to drive on the highway if you were fully cognizant of the fact that you were speeding down the road in a small metal vehicle, surrounded by thousands of other speeding metal vehicles. And if you should be so unfortunate as to become a victim of a crash, you would probably go into shock and remain in that state until you were psychologically capable of handling the reality of what had happened. Psychic numbing is adaptive, or beneficial, when it helps us to *cope* with violence. But it becomes maladaptive, or destructive, when it is used to *enable* violence, even if that violence is as far away as the factories in which animals are turned into food.

Psychic numbing is made up of a complex array of defense mechanisms, mechanisms which are pervasive, powerful, and invisible and which operate on both social and psychological levels. These mechanisms distort our perceptions and distance us from our feelings, transforming our empathy into apathy—indeed, it is the process of learning to not feel that is the focus of this book. The defense mechanisms of psychic numbing include denial, avoidance, routinization, justification, objectification, deindividualization, dichotomization, rationalization, and dissociation. In the upcoming chapters, we'll examine each of these aspects of psychic numbing and deconstruct the system that turns animals into edibles. In so doing, we'll explore the characteristics of this system and the ways in which it ensures our continued support.

NUMBING ACROSS CULTURES AND HISTORY: VARIATIONS ON A THEME

One question I'm often asked is whether people from different cultures and times also have used psychic numbing in order to kill and consume animals. Do tribal hunters, for instance, need to numb themselves when securing their prey? Before the Industrial Revolution, when many people procured their own meat, did they have to emotionally distance themselves from the animals?

It would be impossible to argue that persons from all cultures, in all eras, have employed the same psychic numbing as those of us living in contemporary industrialized societies and who don't need to eat animals to survive. Context determines, in large part, how a person will react to eating animals. One's values, shaped largely by broader social and cultural structures, help determine how much psychological effort must go into distancing oneself from the reality of eating an animal. In societies where meat has been necessary for survival, people haven't had the luxury of reflecting on the ethics of their choices; their values must support eating animals, and they would likely be less distressed at the notion of doing so. How animals are killed, too, affects one's psychological reaction. Cruelty is often more disturbing than killing.

Yet even in instances where eating animals has been a necessity, and the animals have been killed without the gratuitous violence that marks today's slaughterhouses, people have always avoided eating certain types of animals and have consistently striven to reconcile the killing and consumption of those they do consume. Examples abound of rites, rituals, and belief systems that assuage the animal consumer's conscience: the butcher and/or meat eater may perform purification ceremonies after the taking of a life; or an animal may be viewed as "sacrificed" for human consumption, a perspective that imbues the act with spiritual meaning and implies some choice on the part of the prey. Furthermore, as far back as 600 BCE, individuals have chosen to eschew the consumption of meat on ethical grounds, demonstrating a long-standing psychological and moral tension around meat eating. It is certainly possible that psychic numbing has played a role—albeit to varying degrees and in different forms—across cultures and throughout history.[6]

The primary defense of the system is invisibility; invisibility reflects the defenses *avoidance* and *denial* and is the foundation on which all other mechanisms stand. Invisibility enables us, for example, to consume beef without envisioning the animal we're eating; it cloaks our thoughts from ourselves. Invisibility also keeps us safely insulated from the unpleasant process of raising and killing animals for food. The first step in deconstructing eating animals, then, is deconstructing the invisibility of the system, exposing the principles and practices of a system that has since its inception been in hiding.

CHAPTER 2

Carnism:
"It's Just the Way Things Are"

The invisible and the nonexistent look very much alike.
—DELOS B. MCKOWN

The limits of my language mean the limits of my world.
—LUDWIG WITTGENSTEIN

In chapter 1, we did a thought experiment. We imagined that you were at a dinner party, eating a delicious stew, when your friend told you that it contained dog meat. We explored your reactions to that, and then to the fact that your friend said she'd been joking and you were, in fact, eating beef.

Let's try another exercise. Take a moment to think, without self-censoring, of all the words that come to mind when you envision a dog. Next, do the same thing, but this time picture a pig. Now pause and compare your descriptions of these animals. What do you notice? When you thought of a dog, did you think "cute"? "Loyal"? And when you imagined a pig, did you think of "mud" or "sweat"? Did you think "dirty"? If your responses were similar to the ones here, you are in the majority.

I used to teach undergraduate courses in psychology and sociology, and each semester I dedicated one class session to attitudes toward animals. I taught literally thousands of students over the years, and every time we did the aforementioned exercise, the conversation proceeded in essentially the same way, with similar responses.

Just as I asked you to do, I would ask the students to list the characteristics of dogs, and then the characteristics of pigs, and I wrote each list on the board as it was generated. For dogs, the usual adjectives included those we've already covered, as well as "friendly," "intelligent," "fun," "loving," "protective," and sometimes "dangerous." Not surprisingly, pigs got a much less flattering list of descriptives. They were "sweaty" and "dirty," as well as "stupid," "lazy," "fat," and "ugly." Then I had the students explain how they felt toward each of these species. Again, it should come as no surprise that, generally, they at least liked—and often loved—dogs, and were "grossed out" by pigs. Finally, I asked them to describe their relationship to dogs and to pigs. Dogs, of course, were friends and family members, and pigs were food.

At this point the students would start to look perplexed, wondering where our conversation was heading. I then posed a series of questions in response to their previous statements, and the dialogue went something like this:

> So, why do you say pigs are lazy?
> *Because they just lie around all day.*
> Do pigs in the wild do this, or only pigs raised for their meat?
> *I don't know. Maybe when they're on a farm.*
> Why do you think pigs on a farm—or in a factory farm, to be more accurate—lie around?
> *Probably because they're in a pen or cage.*
>
> What makes pigs stupid?
> *They just are.*
> Actually, pigs are considered to be even more intelligent than dogs.

(Sometimes a student would chime in, claiming to have met a pig or to have known someone who had a pig as a pet, and corroborated this with a story or two.)

Why do you say pigs sweat?
No answer.
Did you know that, in fact, pigs don't even have sweat glands?

Are all pigs ugly?
Yes.
What about piglets?
Piglets are cute, but pigs are gross.

Why do you say pigs are dirty?
They roll in mud.

Why do they roll in mud?
Because they like dirt. They're dirty.
Actually, they roll in dirt to cool off when it's hot, since they don't sweat.

Are *dogs* dirty?
Yeah, sometimes. Dogs can do really disgusting things.
Why didn't you include "dirty" in your list for dogs?
Because they're not always dirty. Only sometimes.
Are pigs always dirty?
Yeah, they are.
How do you know this?
Because they always look dirty.
When do you see them?
I don't know. In pictures, I guess.
And they're always dirty in pictures?
No, not always. Pigs aren't always dirty.

You said dogs are loyal, intelligent, and cute. Why do you
say this? How do you know?

I've seen them.

I've lived with dogs.

I've met lots of dogs.

(Inevitably, one or more students would share a story
about a dog who did something particularly heroic,
clever, or adorable.)

What about dogs' feelings? How can you know that dogs
actually feel emotions?

I swear my dog gets depressed when I'm down.

*My dog always got this guilty look and hid under the bed when she
knew she did something wrong.*

Whenever we take my dog to the vet he shakes, he's so scared.

*Our dog used to cry and stop eating when he saw us packing to get
ready to leave for vacation.*

Does anybody here think it's possible that dogs don't
have feelings?

(No hands would be raised.)

What about pigs? Do you think pigs have emotions?

Sure.

Do you think they have the same emotions as dogs?

Maybe. Yeah, I guess.

Actually, most people don't know this, but pigs are so
sensitive that they develop neurotic behaviors, such
as self-mutilation, when in captivity.

Do you think pigs feel pain?

Of course. All animals feel pain.

So why do we eat pigs but not dogs?

Because bacon tastes good. (laughter)

Because dogs have personalities. You can't eat something that has a personality. They have names; they're individuals.

Do you think pigs have personalities? Are they individuals, like dogs?

Yeah, I guess if you get to know them they probably do.

Have you ever met a pig?

(Except for an exceptional student, the majority had not.)

So where did you get your information about pigs from?

Books.

Television.

Ads.

Movies.

I don't know. Society, I guess.

How might you feel about pigs if you thought of them as intelligent, sensitive individuals who are perhaps not sweaty, lazy, and greedy? If you got to know them firsthand, like you know dogs?

I'd feel weird eating them. I'd probably feel kind of guilty.

So why do we eat pigs but not dogs?

Because pigs are bred to be eaten.

Why do we breed pigs to eat them?

I don't know. I never thought about it. I guess, because it's just the way things are.

It's just the way things are. Take a moment to consider this statement. Really think about it. We send one species to the butcher and give our love and kindness to another apparently for no reason other than because *it's the way things are.* When our attitudes and behaviors toward animals are so inconsistent, and this inconsistency is so unexamined, we can safely say we have been fed absurdities. It is absurd that we eat pigs and love dogs and don't even know why. Many of us spend long minutes in the aisle of the drugstore mulling over what toothpaste to buy.

Yet most of us don't spend any time at all thinking about what species of animal we eat and why. Our choices as consumers drive an industry that kills eleven billion* animals per year in the United States alone. If we choose to support this industry and the best reason we can come up with is because it's the way things are, clearly something is amiss. What could cause an entire society of people to check their thinking caps at the door—*and to not even realize they're doing so?* Though this question is quite complex, the answer is quite simple: carnism.

CARNISM

We all know what a vegetarian is—a person who doesn't eat meat. And today many of us know what a vegan is—a person who eschews all animal products. Though some people may choose to become vegan (or vegetarian—the focus of this book, though, is on veganism for reasons that will become clear) to improve their health, many vegans stop eating animals because they don't believe it's ethical to do so. Most of us realize that veganism is often an expression of one's ethical orientation, so when we think of a vegan, we don't simply think of a person who's just like everyone else except that they don't eat animals. We think of a person who has a certain philosophical outlook, whose choice not to eat animals is a reflection of a deeper belief system in which killing animals for human ends is considered unethical. We understand that veganism reflects not merely a dietary orientation, but a way of life. This is why, for instance, when there's a vegan character in a movie, they are depicted not simply as a person who avoids eating meat, eggs, and dairy, but as someone who has a certain set of qualities that we associate with vegans, such as being an animal lover or having unconventional values.

---

* This number does not include the billions of aquatic animals who are also slaughtered annually in the United States.[7]

If a vegan is someone who believes that it's unethical to eat animals, what, then, do we call a person who believes that it's ethical to eat animals? If a vegan is a person who chooses not to eat animals, what is a person who chooses *to* eat animals?

Currently, we use the term "meat eater" to describe anyone who is not vegan or vegetarian. But how accurate is this? As we established, a vegan is not simply a "plant eater." Eating plants is a behavior that stems from a belief system. Both "vegan" and "vegetarian" accurately reflect that a core belief system is at work: the suffix "arian" (shortened to "an" in "vegan") denotes a person who advocates, supports, or practices a doctrine or set of principles.

In contrast, the term "meat eater" isolates the practice of consuming meat, as though it were divorced from a person's beliefs and values. It implies that the person who eats meat is acting *outside* of a belief system. But is eating meat truly a behavior that exists independent of a belief system? Do we eat pigs but not dogs because we don't have a belief system when it comes to eating animals?

In much of the industrialized world, we eat animals not because we have to; we eat animals because we choose to. We don't need to eat animals to survive or even to be healthy; millions of healthy and long-lived vegans have proven this point. We eat animals simply because it's what we've always done, and because we like the way they taste. Most of us eat animals because it's just the way things are.

We don't see meat eating as we do veganism—as a choice, based on a set of assumptions about animals, our world, and ourselves. Rather, we see it as a given, the "natural" thing to do, the way things have always been and the way things will always be. We eat animals without thinking about what we are doing and why because the belief system that underlies this behavior is invisible. This invisible belief system is what I call *"carnism."*

Carnism is the belief system that conditions us to eat certain animals. We sometimes think of those who eat animals as carnivores. But carnivores are, by definition, animals that are dependent on meat to survive. Those who consume animals are also not merely omnivores. An omnivore is an animal—human or nonhuman—that has the physiological ability to ingest both plants and meat. Both "carnivore," "omnivore" are terms that describe one's biological constitution, not one's philosophical choice. In much of the world today people eat animals not because they need to, but because they choose to, and choices always stem from beliefs.

Carnism's invisibility accounts for why choices appear not to be choices at all. But why has carnism remained invisible in the first place? Why haven't we named it? There's a very good reason for this. It's because carnism is a particular type of belief system, an *ideology*, and it's also a particular type of ideology, one that is especially resistant to scrutiny. Let's look at each of these features of carnism in turn.

If the problem is invisible . . .
then there will be ethical invisibility.
—CAROL J. ADAMS

CARNISM, IDEOLOGY, AND THE STATUS QUO

An ideology is a shared set of beliefs, as well as the practices that reflect these beliefs. For instance, feminism is an ideology. Feminists are people who believe that women deserve to be viewed and treated as equals to men. Because men make up the dominant social group—the group that holds power in society—feminists challenge male dominance on every front, from the home to the political arena. Feminist ideology forms the basis of feminist beliefs and practices.

It's fairly easy to recognize feminism as an ideology, just as it's easy to understand that veganism isn't simply about not eating animals. Both "feminist" and "vegan" conjure up images of a person who has a certain set of beliefs, someone who isn't just like everybody else.

So what about "everybody else"? What about the majority, the mainstream, all the "normal" people? Where do their beliefs come from?

We tend to view the mainstream way of life as a reflection of universal values. Yet what we consider normal is, in fact, nothing more than the beliefs and behaviors of the majority. Before the scientific revolution, for example, mainstream European beliefs held that the sky was made up of heavenly spheres that revolved around the earth, that the earth was the exalted center of the universe. This belief was so ingrained that to proclaim otherwise, as did Copernicus, and later Galileo, was to risk death. So what we refer to as mainstream is simply another way to describe an ideology that is so widespread—so *entrenched*—that its assumptions and practices are seen as simply common sense. It is considered fact rather than opinion, its practices a given rather than a choice. It's the norm. It's the way things are. And it's the reason carnism has not been named until now.

When an ideology is entrenched, it is essentially invisible. An example of an invisible ideology is *patriarchy*, the ideology in which masculinity is valued over femininity and in which men therefore have more social power than women. Consider, for instance, which of the following qualities are most likely to make someone socially and financially successful: assertiveness, passivity, competitiveness, sharing, control, authority, power, rationality, emotionality, independence, dependence, nurturance, vulnerability. Chances are you chose the qualities that are masculine, and you didn't realize that your choices reflect patriarchal values; most of us don't see patriarchy as an ideology that teaches us to think and act a certain way. People of all genders simply accept that it's better to be, for example, more rational and less emotional, even though both of these qualities are equally necessary for our well-being.

Patriarchy existed for thousands of years before feminists named this ideology. So, too, has been the case with carnism. Interestingly, the ideology of vegetarianism was named more than 2,500 years ago; those who chose not to eat meat were called "Pythagoreans," because they followed the dietary philosophy of the ancient Greek philosopher and mathematician, Pythagoras. Later, in the nineteenth century, the term "vegetarian" was coined, followed by the term "vegan" in 1944. But only now, centuries after labeling those who don't eat animals, has the ideology of eating animals been named.

In some ways it only makes sense that vegetarianism and veganism were named before carnism. It's easier to recognize those ideologies that fall outside the mainstream. But there is another, more important, reason that vegetarianism and veganism have been labeled while carnism has not. The primary way entrenched ideologies stay entrenched is by remaining invisible. And the primary way they stay invisible is by remaining unnamed. If we don't name an ideology, we can't talk about it, and if we can't talk about it, we can't question it.

Whatever is unnamed, undepicted in images . . . whatever is misnamed as something else, made difficult-to-come-by, whatever is buried in the memory by the collapse of meaning under an inadequate or lying language—this will become, not merely unspoken, but unspeakable.
—ADRIENNE RICH

CARNISM, IDEOLOGY, AND VIOLENCE

While it is difficult, if not impossible, to question an ideology that we don't even know exists, it's even more difficult when that ideology actively works to keep itself hidden. This is the case with ideologies such as carnism. Carnism is a violent ideology; if we were to remove the violence from the system—to stop harming and killing animals—the system would cease to exist. (Another name for violent ideology is *system of oppression,* or *oppressive system.*)

Contemporary carnism is organized around extensive violence. This level of violence is necessary in order to process and slaughter enough animals for carnistic industry to maintain its current profit margin. The violence of carnism is such that most people are unwilling to witness it, and those who do can become seriously distraught. In my classes, before showing a film on animal agriculture, I had to take a number of measures to ensure that the psychological environment was safe enough to expose students to footage that would inevitably cause them distress. And I have personally worked with numerous vegan advocates who suffer from post-traumatic stress disorder (PTSD) as the result of prolonged exposure to the processing and slaughter of animals; they have intrusive thoughts, nightmares, flashbacks, difficulty concentrating, anxiety, insomnia, and a host of other symptoms. In close to three decades of speaking and teaching about animal agriculture, I have yet to see a person who doesn't cringe when witnessing how animals are turned into food. People generally hate to see animals suffer.

Why do we hate to see animals in pain? Because we feel for other sentient beings. Most of us, even those who are not "animal lovers" per se, don't want to cause anyone—human or nonhuman—to suffer, especially if that suffering is intensive and unnecessary. It is for this reason that violent ideologies must use defense mechanisms that enable compassionate people to support cruel practices and to not even realize what they're doing.

UNNATURAL BORN KILLERS

There is a substantial body of evidence demonstrating humans' seemingly natural aversion to killing. Much of the research in this area has been conducted by the military; analysts have found that soldiers tend to intentionally fire over the enemy's head, or not to fire at all.[8]

Studies of combat activity during the Napoleonic and Civil wars revealed striking statistics. Given the ability of the men, their proximity to the enemy, and the capacity of their weapons, the number of enemy soldiers hit should have been well over 50 percent, resulting in a killing rate of hundreds per minute. Instead, however, the hit rate was only one or two per minute. And a similar phenomenon occurred during World War I: according to British lieutenant George Roupell, the only way he could get his men to stop firing into the air was by drawing his sword, walking down the trench, "beating [them] on the backside and . . . telling them to fire low."[9]

World War II fire rates were also remarkably low: historian and US Army brigadier general S. L. A. Marshall reported that, during battle, the firing rate was a mere 15 to 20 percent; in other words, out of every hundred men engaged in a firefight, only fifteen to twenty actually used their weapons. And in Vietnam, for every enemy soldier killed, more than fifty thousand bullets were fired.[10]

What these studies have taught the military is that in order to get soldiers to shoot to kill, to actively participate in violence, the soldiers must be sufficiently desensitized to the act of killing. In other words, they have to *learn to not feel*—and to not feel responsible—for their actions. They must be taught to override their own conscience. Yet these studies also demonstrate that even in the face of immediate danger, in situations of extreme violence, most people are averse to killing. In other words, as Marshall concludes, "the vast majority of combatants throughout history, at the moment of truth when they could and should kill the enemy, have found themselves to be 'conscientious objectors.'"[11]

As I mentioned in chapter 1, the primary defense of carnism is invisibility. We've already discussed how carnism is socially and psychologically invisible. But violent ideologies also depend on physical invisibility; their violence is well hidden from public scrutiny. Have you ever noticed that, though we breed, raise, and kill eleven billion animals per year, most of us never see even a single part of the process of carnistic production?

Once we genuinely think about the meat, eggs, and dairy we eat, once we realize that there is much more to our culinary tastes than our own natural, unadulterated preferences, then "it's just the way things are" is simply not a good enough explanation for why we eat pigs but not dogs. Let's turn now and have a look at the way things really are.

CHAPTER 3

The Way Things *Really* Are

Make the lie big, make it simple, keep saying it, and eventually they will believe it.

—ADOLF HITLER*

If you are like most people, meat, eggs, and dairy are staples of your diet. You probably eat these products multiple times a day. Think about the foods you've eaten over the past week. How many meals have you had that consisted of some form of chicken, beef, pork, or fish? Have you had eggs or yogurt for your breakfast? Turkey or tuna sandwiches for lunch? Rotisserie or fried chicken for dinner? How much meat, eggs, and dairy do you think you've eaten this week? This month? This year?

The US Department of Agriculture (USDA) estimates that the average American consumes 92 pounds of chicken,[12] 16 pounds of turkey,[13] 57 pounds of beef,[14] and 51 pounds of pork per year. Add to this a pound of veal and a pound of lamb, and each of us eats a total of 222 pounds[15] of meat annually[16]—and that's not even counting the 16 pounds of fish,[17] 37 pounds of eggs, and 630 pounds of dairy products we consume. Given that the current population of the United States is 328 million, that's a lot of meat, eggs, and dairy— and a lot of animals. (And this level of carnistic consumption is not uniquely American. For example, in the EU, people eat an annual average of 115 kg of poultry, 110 kg of fish, 105

---

* attributed

kg of dairy, 96 kg of pork products, 86 kg of beef and 13 kg of eggs;[18] and numbers are similar elsewhere in the world.)

To be exact, US agribusinesses slaughter *eleven billion* animals per year[19] (and that's not including the estimated 47 billion fish and other aquatic animals killed annually[20]). That's 23,234 animals per minute, or 387 animals per second. In the time it took you to read these three paragraphs, nearly 73,000 more animals were killed.

Just to give you some perspective, the eleven billion US farmed animal population is nearly double the size of the worldwide human population. It's 33 times larger than the population of New York City, and 2,750 times larger than the population of Los Angeles.

Another way to think about this number is that if we were to try to pack eleven billion people into a football field, it would take 121,000 football fields—an area about the size of Los Angeles—to hold them all. Or if eleven billion people stood in a line, the line would be 2.2 million miles long. That's long enough to reach to the moon and back, nearly five times. It's also long enough to wrap around the entire circumference of the earth 83 times. And we're only talking about the number of animals killed in a single year; consider how these numbers increase over five, ten, twenty years.

Obviously, it takes a lot of animals to produce the amount of meat, eggs, and dairy we, as a nation, buy, sell, and consume. Animal agriculture is big business. In fact, animal agriculture is very big business—US carnistic industries have combined annual revenues approaching $177 billion[21] (a similar amount as that of the EU).[22] Consider the countless grocery stores, restaurants, cafeterias, and homes across the country that are stocked with carnistic products. Meat, eggs, and dairy are literally everywhere we turn.

So where are all the animals?

WHERE ARE THEY?

Of the eleven billion animals who have been raised, transported, and slaughtered over the course of the past year, how many have you seen? If you live in a city, probably almost none. But let's assume you live in the country. How many cows do you see grazing on the hillsides? Perhaps fifty at a time, if that? And how about chickens or pigs or turkeys? Do you see any at all? How many times have you seen these animals on television, in magazines and newspapers, in the movies? Though we may eat them on a daily basis, most of us don't stop to consider how peculiar it is that we can go through our entire lives without ever encountering the animals who become our food. Where are they?

The vast majority of the animals we eat are not, as those in carnistic industry would have us believe, "contented cows" and "happy hens" lazing amid grassy fields and open barnyards. They are not sleeping in spacious stalls with fresh hay. From the moment they are born, these individuals are kept in intensive confinement where they may suffer from disease, exposure to extreme temperatures, severe overcrowding, violent handling, and even psychosis. Despite what the prevailing imagery of farmed animals suggests, small, family-run farms are largely a thing of the past; today the animals are in massive "confined animal feeding operations," or CAFOs (sometimes called "factory farms"), where they reside until they are shipped to the slaughterhouse.*

As with any major production facility, CAFOs (and the slaughterhouses they supply) are designed with a singular intention: to manufacture their product at the lowest cost and for the highest profit possible. Quite simply, the more animals processed and killed per minute, the more money to be made. Toward this end, CAFOs may house up to a

---

* The general practices described in this book are similar around the world, even though legislation affecting specific procedures sometimes differs.

million animals at a time,[23] animals who are viewed and treated as units of production and whose welfare is necessarily secondary to the profit their bodies will turn. From a business standpoint, animal welfare is a *barrier* to profit, as it costs less to mass-produce animals and discard those who die prematurely than it does to care for them adequately. In fact, it is estimated that upward of two billion animals destined to become food die before reaching the slaughterhouse,[24] a factor that is built into the cost of production. It is these cost-cutting measures that make modern carnistic production one of the most violent practices in human history.

SEE NO EVIL, HEAR NO EVIL, SPEAK NO EVIL

The most effective way to distort reality is to deny it; if we tell ourselves there isn't a problem, then we never have to worry about what to do about it. And the most effective way to deny a reality is to make it invisible. As we've discussed, invisibility is the bulwark of the carnistic system.

In chapter 2 we deconstructed the *symbolic* invisibility of the system. Symbolic invisibility is enabled by the defense mechanism *avoidance*, which is a form of denial. We avoid the truth when we avoid naming the system, which, in turn, prevents us from realizing that there even *is* a system. In this chapter, we will deconstruct the *practical* invisibility of carnism. This deconstruction is necessary in order to truly appreciate the mechanisms and dynamics of carnism. As long as we are uninformed or misinformed, we cannot understand the reality of carnistic production and move beyond carnistic defenses.

The establishments that produce the bulk of the meat, eggs, and dairy that make it to our dinner plates are, essentially, invisible. We don't see them. We don't see them because they are located in remote areas where most of us don't venture. We don't see them because we're not allowed access even if we do try to get in.[25] We don't see them because their trucks are often sealed and unmarked. We don't see them because, as Erik Schlosser, investigative author of the bestselling *Fast Food Nation*, says, they have "no windows on the front and no architectural clues to what's happening inside."[26] *We don't see them because we're not supposed to.* As with any violent ideology, the populace must be shielded from direct exposure to the victims of the system, lest they begin questioning the system or their participation in it. This truth speaks for itself: why else would carnistic industry go to such lengths to keep its practices invisible?

ACCESS DENIED

In 2007,* journalist Daniel Zwerdling set out to write an article on the chicken industry for *Gourmet* magazine. Given the industry's response to his request for a tour of their plants, one would think Zwerdling was writing for *Vegetarian Times* rather than a renowned publication of carnistic cuisine. According to Zwerdling, whose article "A View to a Kill" was published in the June issue, "Spokesmen at the five biggest companies refused to show me the farms where their suppliers raise the chickens you eat, so that I could see firsthand how they treat them. They refused to show me the slaughterhouses, so I could see how the companies dispatch them. Executives even refused to talk to me about how they raise and kill chickens." And Zwerdling's experience is not uncommon.

---

* I have retained some older sources that I used for the original edition of this book because the information they contain is still relevant.

Not only is it difficult to obtain access to meat-packing plants, but in a number of states it's actually against the law to take photos or videos inside "animal enterprises," such as laboratories, circuses, and slaughterhouses. Furthermore, the Animal Enterprise Terrorism Act of 2006—legislation that has been harshly criticized as unconstitutional—makes it *illegal to engage in behavior that results in the economic disruption of an animal enterprise.*[27]

Because the media is denied access to "animal enterprises," most of the footage of CAFOs and slaughterhouses that reaches the public comes from undercover investigations. Such was the case with the 2008 Humane Society of the United States (HSUS) investigation that documented workers dragging sick dairy cows with chains and flipping them with forklifts—to be processed into meat destined for public school cafeterias—that led to the largest recall of beef in the nation's history.

THIS LITTLE PIGGY
WENT TO MARKET . . .

As we discussed in chapter 2, pigs are intelligent, sensitive animals; piglets as young as three weeks old learn their names and respond when called. In fact, research from Pennsylvania State University revealed that pigs could be trained to play computer games; using their snouts to control joysticks, they were able to hit their targets with 80-percent accuracy.[28] Pigs are also affectionate and sociable, enjoying the company of humans, which is why they can make excellent companion animals. Several years ago, I visited a shelter for rescued farmed animals, and the pigs couldn't get enough of my scratching their bellies and behind their ears.

In natural settings, pigs roam for up to thirty miles a day and can form close bonds with one another. They may be able to distinguish between as many as thirty different individual pigs in their group, and will greet and communicate with those with whom they are close. Expectant mothers are extremely conscientious; they may wander for six miles to find the perfect spot to build a birthing nest, and then spend up to ten hours building it before settling in to care for their newborns. Once the babies are old enough to rejoin the others, they play and explore their environment together for months.[29]

Most pigs, however—approximately 80 million[30]—spend their entire lives in intensive confinement and never see the outdoors until they are packed into trucks to be sent to slaughter. Shortly after piglets are born, they are typically castrated, and their tails are cut off, without anesthesia. Ranchers are told to remove ("dock") their tails with blunt, side-cutting pliers because the crushing action helps to reduce bleeding.[31] Tail docking is necessary because under extreme stress and when all their natural urges have been thwarted, pigs develop neurotic behaviors and can actually bite each others' tails off.[32] This psychological reaction is one of the symptoms of what is referred to in the industry as porcine stress syndrome (PSS), a condition that is remarkably similar to what we call in humans post-traumatic stress disorder (PTSD). Other symptoms include rigidity, panting, anxiety, blotchy skin, and sometimes sudden death.[33] Like humans who have endured solitary confinement and other tortures in captivity, pigs have engaged in self-harm, and have been found repeating the same nonsensical behaviors over and over, sometimes thousands of times a day; the animals are literally driven insane.*

---

* The technical term for repetitive behaviors is *stereotypies*. Stereotypies are a symptom of stress seen in a number of animal species (e.g., large cats pacing in a cage at the zoo), but they are not classified as a symptom of PSS.

OF PIGS AND PEOPLE:
THE GENETICS OF TRAUMA

Post-traumatic stress disorder (PTSD) and porcine stress syndrome (PSS) seem to share a genetic basis; both conditions are in part hereditary. A number of studies have revealed that a person's genetic predisposition, combined with a traumatic experience, increases the likelihood of developing PTSD; a large study of twin Vietnam veterans, for instance, led researchers to claim that there is "a significant genetic contribution to PTSD." Similarly, the Ontario Ministry of Agriculture, Food and Rural Affairs reports that it is the combination of genetics and stress that leads to the development of PSS in pigs.[34]

Piglets born in confinement are allowed to suckle for just two to three weeks,[35] and they do this through the bars of a crate that is separate from their mother's. A number of piglets die before being weaned, from maladies such as starvation or diarrhea.[36] Sometimes if a piglet has managed to squeeze into their mother's crate to satisfy their instinctive need for warmth and closeness, the mother can accidentally crush them. Regardless of the cause, infant deaths are inevitable. There are simply too many animals for workers to care for adequately; a typical hog breeding plant employs four people to manage 3,200 sows.[37]

After weaning, for the next six months, the young pigs are crammed into what are often filthy pens or sheds in hog factories.[38] These buildingscare filled with noxious gases from the pigs' excrement, and the air is dense with dust and dander. Both pigs and the humans who work in pig confinement buildings suffer from chronic respiratory illnesses, and a number of pigs die prematurely from lung disease.[39]

When the pigs are ready to be slaughtered, they are herded onto tractors bound for the slaughterhouse. To save money, as many pigs as possible are packed into a truck, and this overcrowding—coupled with the fact that the animals receive no food, water, or protection from extreme temperatures during transport, which can last upwards of twenty-eight hours[40]—results in high mortality rates; according to *The National Hog Farmer*, an industry publication, "The national recorded incidence for dead on arrival (DOA) pigs [in 2007] was 0.21%. Based on 22 commercial field trials, the rate of non-ambulatory pigs (classified as fatigued or injured) prior to reaching the weigh scale at the packing plant was about 0.37%. No national figures exist for non-ambulatory pigs."[41] Agricultural investigator Gail Eisnitz, who interviewed a number of slaughterhouse workers, was told of the transport process:

> You're going to lose hogs in a semitrailer no matter what . . . .
>
> During the time I worked in rendering, there was large piles of dead hogs every day. . . . When they come off the truck, they're solid as a block of ice. . . . I went to pick up some hogs one day for chainsawing from a pile of about thirty frozen hogs, and I found two [that were] frozen but still alive I could tell they were alive because they raised their heads up like, "Help me." . . . I took my ax-chopper and chopped them to death.[42]

The pigs who do survive the journey are deposited into holding pens to await slaughter.[43] When it is time, they are prodded onto a narrow walkway, or chute, on which they walk single file to the killing floor. The animals at the rear of the chute hear the screams of the pigs ahead, who have arrived at the slaughter line, as well as the shouts of men working on the noisy production line. Schlosser explains what he saw upon reaching this point in his tour: "The sounds get louder—factory sounds, the noise of power tools and machinery, bursts of compressed air . . . . We walk up a slippery metal stairway and reach a small platform, where the production line begins. A man turns and smiles at me. He wears safety goggles and a hard hat. His face is splattered with gray matter and blood."[44] Not surprisingly, many pigs are reluctant to move forward. As one slaughterhouse worker put it:

> When the hogs smell blood, they don't want to go. I've seen hogs beaten, whipped, kicked in the head to get them up to the restrainer. One night I saw a driver get so angry at a hog he broke its back with a piece of a board. I've seen hog drivers take their prod and shove it up the hog's ass to get them to move. I didn't appreciate that because it made the hogs twice as wild by the time they got to me.[45]

Farmed animals are supposed to be stunned and rendered unconscious before they are actually killed.[46] However, some pigs remain conscious when they are strung upside down by their legs in shackles, and they kick and struggle as they are moved along the conveyor belt to have their throats slit. Because of the speed at which the animals are supposed to be stunned and killed, and because slaughterhouse workers are often ineffectively trained, a number of pigs may also survive throat cutting and remain conscious when they arrive at the next station, where they are dropped into scalding water—a procedure done to remove their hair. Eisnitz describes how squealing hogs were left dangling by one leg while workers left to take their lunch breaks, and thousands of hogs were immersed in the scalding tank alive. And one worker she interviewed commented: "These hogs . . . hit the water and start screaming and kicking. Sometimes they thrash so much they kick water out of the tank. There's a rotating arm that pushes them under, no chance for them to get out. I'm not sure if they burn to death before they drown, but it takes them a couple of minutes to stop thrashing."[47]

Eisnitz also found that the stress workers faced from spending hours at a single station where they had to kill (or stun) one hog every four seconds led to violent outbursts toward the pigs. One worker described such an incident:

> Like, one day the live hogs were driving me nuts [when] an animal pisses you off [even though you] are going to kill it. . . . Only you don't just kill it, you go in hard, push hard, blow the windpipe, make it drown in its own blood. Split its nose. A live hog would be running around the pit. It would just be looking up at me and I'd be sticking and I would just take my knife and cut its eye out while it was just sitting there. And this hog would just scream. One time I took my knife—it's sharp enough—and I sliced off the end of a hog's nose, just like a piece of bologna. The hog went crazy for a few seconds. Then it just sat there looking kind of stupid. So I took a handful of salt brine and ground it into its nose. Now that hog really went nuts, brushing its nose all over the place. I still had a bunch of salt left on my hand—I was wearing a rubber glove—and I stuck the salt right up the hog's ass. The poor hog didn't know whether to shit or go blind.[48]

Female pigs who are used as breeders eventually wind up at the slaughterhouse as well, but before that time they spend much of their lives in small metal cages and stalls that are referred to as gestation crates.[*49] These crates are two feet wide, too small for the sows to even turn around, and their floors are covered in feces and urine. The animals suffer from a number of problems due to this confinement, but one of the most painful conditions they endure is urinary tract infections, which can be become so severe as to be fatal. Urinary tract infections occur because when the sows lie down, they are immersed in bacteria ridden waste that makes its way into their urinary tracts. A sow will be forcibly impregnated in rapid cycles of every five or six months, until she is no longer able to reproduce, at which time she is packed onto a truck headed for slaughter.[50]

"WHOEVER DEFINES THE ISSUE CONTROLS THE DEBATE"

Timothy Cummings, a poultry veterinarian and clinical professor at Mississippi State University, explained to an audience of poultry producers that it's time to take on media-savvy animal rights advocates who understand the power of language. "Whoever defines the issue controls the debate," he said.[52] Cummings suggested that "debeaking" a chicken should instead be called "beak conditioning," making the process seem more like a spa treatment than a disfiguration. The "backup killer" (the worker responsible for slaughtering birds who are still alive after passing the automatic killer) should be a "knife operator," and the term "insanguinated" should replace "bled" to death.

---

* Gestation crates have been considered so inhumane that they've been banned in a number of states and nations. The European Union banned them in 2013, and both Smithfield Foods[51] and Maple Leaf Foods, the largest pork producers in the United States and Canada, have wholly or partially banned (or said they would ban) their use as well.

Industry insiders have long been aware of the discomfort consumers feel when words paint too accurate a picture of how animals are turned into food. As far back as 1922, the Texas Sheep and Goat Raisers' Association proposed replacing "goat meat" with "chevron," arguing that: "People don't eat ground cow, pig chops, or leg of sheep . . . beef, pork, and mutton sound much more appetizing."[53] And the former National Cattlemen's Beef Association advised its members to substitute "process" or "harvest" for "slaughter," since "people react negatively to the word 'slaughtering.'"[54]

In the United Kingdom, too, one can find interesting examples of how carnistic industry uses language to camouflage the reality of its products. The *Meat Trades Journal* advises readers to use "meat plant" or "meat factory" in lieu of "slaughterhouse."[55] And *Meat* issued the following statement: "Traditional retailing centres around offering the public bits of animals and often identifies meat with livestock. But modern consumer attitudes shy away from this link. There is an urgent need for a new retailing philosophy. We are no longer in the business of selling pieces of carcase meat. We must make our customers think forward to what they will eat rather than backwards to the animal in the field."[56]

WHERE'S THE BEEF?

Michael Pollan traced the life of a single steer, steer number 534, in order to write *The Omnivore's Dilemma,* his bestselling exposé on contemporary food-production practices. What Pollan found when he followed steer number 534 from birth to death represents the fate of the 35 million steers who are killed every year in the United States for beef. Pollan describes how he was surveying a herd of calves in a pen when "534 moseyed up to the railing and made eye contact. He had a wide stout frame and was brockle-faced. Here was my boy."[57]

It isn't surprising that 534 so readily approached Pollan. Bovines are communicative, emotional, and social creatures. They have multiple vocalizations and gestures to communicate their feelings, and in a natural environment they will nurture ongoing friendships with one another. Bovines are naturally gentle and docile, spending most of their waking time eating grass and chewing cud. And babies frequently engage in a variety of forms of play with each other when they are not suckling from their mothers.

Bovines born into captivity are unable to satisfy many of these natural instincts. However, for a short time, at least some of their basic needs are met. Unlike the pork and poultry industries, the beef industry keeps its animals outdoors for the first six months of their lives (which, however, also means enduring extreme temperatures and weather),[58] since it is cheaper to contract independent ranchers who own grazing land to manage this part of the process. Pollan reports: "Steer number 534 spent his first six months in these lush pastures alongside his mother, 9534. Apart from the trauma of the Saturday in April when he was branded and castrated, one could imagine 534 looking back on those six months as the good old days."[59]

Steer 534 had been born in the birthing shed across the street from the pasture, and like all male calves, his castration, branding, and "de-horning" (to prevent his horns from getting stuck in fences or causing harm to other animals or humans) took place without anesthesia. Agriculturalists at the University of Tennessee explain the most efficient ways to perform some of the different methods of castrating calves.[60] Stress from the procedures, they say, can be "minimized by performing the procedure when the calf is small and sexually immature." One method involves using a knife to cut off the lower part of the scrotum: "After the testicles are exposed, they should be grasped and extended one at a time while pushing back the connective tissue surrounding the cord. In young calves, the testicle may be grasped and pulled until the cord breaks." Or operators can place a rubber band on the scrotum above the testicles: "This cuts off the blood supply and the scrotum and testicles slough off in about three weeks." However, they warn, "This is the least desirable of all the bloodless methods of castration because of the danger of tetanus. If this method is used, it should be used on calves less than one month of age." Another bloodless method of castration involves the use of an *emasculatome,* an instrument with blunt blades that crush the spermatic cord and sever the blood supply: "The emasculatome is left in place for approximately one minute. It is strongly suggested that the emasculatome be applied twice on each cord. Repeat the procedure on the other side of the scrotum. . . . If the cord has been missed, repeat the procedure." And finally, the agriculturalists advise that "[t]he best times to castrate are in the spring and fall when flies and maggots are less likely to increase irritation and infection of the wound."

Given these castration practices, it is not surprising that Pollan believes 534 was traumatized. Pollan claims that 534 was traumatized a second time, as well, when he was weaned from his mother at six months of age: "Weaning is perhaps the most traumatic time on a ranch for animals and ranchers alike; cows separated from their calves will bellow for days, and the calves, stressed, are prone to getting sick."[61] Weaning is recognized as a major psychological stressor by agricultural veterinarians, who therefore recommend that the facilities that hold both mother and calf after they have been separated should be strong enough to prevent the two from being able to reunite.[62]

After weaning, 534 was sent off to spend the next couple of months in a "backgrounding" pen, where he was to get used to confinement, eating from a trough, and consuming unnatural foods—which were comprised of massive quantities of drug-ridden corn, and protein and fat supplements to bring him from 80 to 1,200 pounds in eleven months.[63] The rest of his life would be spent in a feedlot, an overcrowded, filthy, factory farm with flooring largely comprised of manure, where he would be confined with thousands of other steers awaiting slaughter.[64]

When it comes time for slaughter, steers are no more eager to walk the chute to the kill floor than are pigs. They must be prodded along, a process that further stresses already frustrated animals and workers. Though under federal law it is illegal to use prods in excess of fifty volts, one employee Eisnitz interviewed commented:

> You can get frustrated when you're trying to move cattle along. Sometimes you have to prod them a lot. But some of the drivers [people who prod cattle along the chute] burn the hell out of them. The five or six hotshots (electric prods) by the lead-up chutes are hooked directly to a 110-volt outlet. Run them along the floor's metal grates and they spit sparks like a welding machine. Some drivers would beat cattle with hotshots until they were so wild and panicky you couldn't do a thing with them, right up into the knocking box.[65]

Once at the assembly line, the steers are stunned, shackled, bled, disemboweled, and skinned. As with hogs, the lack of skilled workers and the dizzying speed of the conveyor belt prevent precision in stunning, and many steers end up being pulled along while conscious. Conscious steers on the line are particularly dangerous for workers, because, at 1,000 pounds, when they thrash and kick, they can sometimes break free from the shackles and fall headfirst onto employees from a height of fifteen feet. Even when the animal is directly stunned, sometimes it takes multiple times for the hit to render him unconscious. Another employee commented:

> I remember one bull with really long horns. I knocked it twice. . . . Some solid white stuff came out—brains, I guess—and it went down, its face all bloody. I rolled it into the shackling area. That bull must have felt the shackle going on its leg, it got up like nothing ever happened to it, it didn't even wobble, and took off out the back door, started running down Route 17 and just wouldn't stop. They went out and shot it with a rifle, dragged it back with the tractor.[66]

Schlosser, too, witnessed the effects of inadequate stunning: "A steer slips from its chain, falls to the ground, and gets its head caught in a conveyor belt. The line stops as workers struggle to free the steer, stunned but alive, from the machinery. I've seen enough."[67]

Pollan was not permitted entry to the kill floor, so he awaited the arrival of his steer at the final destination of his journey. There, 534 emerged as a box of steaks. No longer even a number, 534 had been reduced to a container of neatly packaged products destined for supermarket shelves.

THEY DIE PIECE BY PIECE

In 2001, the Washington Post printed an article by Joby Warrick entitled "They Die Piece by Piece." Warrick explained how, though steers were supposed to be dead before reaching the cutting room, this was often not the reality. Ramon Moreno, a slaughterhouse worker who'd spent twenty years as a "second-legger"—cutting hocks off carcasses as they sped past at the rate of 309 per hour—described the process to Warrick: "'They blink. They make noises,' he said softly. 'The head moves, the eyes are wide and looking around.' Still Moreno would cut. On bad days, he says, dozens of animals reached his station clearly alive and conscious. Some would survive as far as the tail cutter, the belly ripper, the hide puller. 'They die,' said Moreno, 'piece by piece.'"[68]

BIRD BRAINS?
CHICKENS AND TURKEYS

In chapter 2, I discussed some of the common assumptions we make about pigs and how these beliefs make it easier for us to eat them. Many of us feel even more removed from chickens and turkeys, at least in part because of our deep-rooted belief that they are stupid—perhaps too stupid to even know whether they are in pain. However, birds are actually quite smart; scientists now acknowledge that these animals are vastly more intelligent than they'd realized.[69] Chickens and turkeys are also quite sociable, which may explain the growing trend of keeping them as pets. Those who keep pet chickens or turkeys describe birds who play with them, seek them out for affection, and even cavort with the family dog. There are also websites dedicated exclusively to living with companion birds. For instance, at *mypetchicken.com*, proud "bird owners" can post pictures of their favorite chickens for all to admire.

Nevertheless, in the United States we kill and consume approximately nine billion birds a year for their flesh or eggs.[70] "Broiler" chickens and turkeys are raised for their meat, and though in natural conditions they live up to ten years, in CAFOs they have a life span of seven weeks or sixteen weeks, respectively—which means that, whenever we consume poultry, we are, in fact, eating baby birds. The birds' severely shortened life span is largely due to both selective breeding and their being fed a diet so full of growth-promoting drugs[71] that they grow at double the speed they would naturally. For this reason, these birds suffer from numerous structural deformities. Their legs are unable to hold their weight and are often twisted and broken; they cannot move much due to chronic joint pain. And when it comes time to be shipped to slaughter, as they are grabbed and crammed into crates that are stacked on top of one another, they can suffer broken or dislocated wings, hips, and legs, as well as internal hemorrhages.[72]

Birds raised for meat spend their lives in barren sheds— or "broiler houses"—that typically hold 20,000 animals at a time, with more modern facilities holding even larger numbers of individuals,[73] and which are so crowded it is difficult to see the floor. In these conditions, the birds are unable to carry out any of their natural behaviors, such as foraging and roosting, and they develop psychotic, stress-induced behaviors, such as feather pecking and cannibalism. Often, in order to prevent them from pecking each other to death, a hot blade is used to cut off the front part of their beaks, without anesthesia, at birth. This procedure, known as debeaking, can lead to infection, the growth of neurological tumors, or death if the bird doesn't have enough of a beak left to use for drinking or eating.[74]

The birds that survive the broiler house are then sent to slaughter. In poultry slaughterhouses, where production speeds are even faster than those for other animals (the average is 8,400 animals per hour),[75] birds are thrown onto conveyors where they are grabbed, sometimes handfuls of them at a time, and hooked upside down on shackles. While the Humane Methods of Slaughter Act requires other animals to be rendered unconscious before being killed, birds are exempt and are slaughtered while fully conscious. Their throats are slit by either hand or machine, and they are then dumped into scalding water to loosen their feathers. A number of birds end up being boiled alive.

Josh Balk, an activist who had worked undercover at a Perdue chicken slaughter plant in 2004 before becoming a director at the Humane Society of the United States, spoke with me about his experience at the plant. He also videotaped and published his accounts of the experience, in particular the workers' ongoing aggression toward the birds. Balk kept a daily log,[76] and following are excerpts:

> Nearly every chicken responded with screams and violent physical reactions from the moment they were grabbed by workers and as they went through the line. The screaming of the birds and the frenzied flapping of their wings were so loud that you had to yell to the worker next to you, who was standing less than two feet away, just so he could hear you.

> I saw an employee kick a chicken off the floor fan and routinely saw chickens being thrown around the room. . . . While one of the workers was talking about football, he "spiked" a chicken onto the conveyer belt, pretending he had scored a touchdown.

> I saw about 50 birds being dumped from the transport crates onto the conveyer belt, a distance of approximately eight feet. The crate tipped them all at once, so they fell on top of each other. The screaming was intense during the whole process. I looked onto the conveyer belt and could clearly see chickens with broken legs and wings, limbs sticking out in unnatural angles.

> I . . . noticed that our line leader seemed generally more hostile toward the birds today, even yelling profanities at them when he threw them. During one

break, a worker repeatedly slapped a chicken in the face until the line started again.

There were so many dead birds on the floor of the hanging room that it was difficult to take a step without stepping on one.

As with other species destined for human consumption, the public is shielded from witnessing the lives and deaths of some nine billion chickens per year. As Balk explained, "Being there firsthand to hear the screams and to smell the stench of death in the air is something that most people would never . . . experience."

CAN THEY SUFFER?

Calling for the humane treatment of animals, seventeenth-century philosopher Jeremy Bentham argued, "The question is not, 'Can they reason?' nor, 'Can they talk?' but rather, 'Can they suffer?'" The question of sentience—the ability to feel pleasure and pain—has been at the center of arguments surrounding both human and animal welfare.

Historically, members of vulnerable groups have been believed to have a higher tolerance for pain, an assumption often invoked to justify suffering. For instance, fifteenth-century scientists would nail dogs to boards by their paws in order to cut them open and experiment on them while fully conscious, and they dismissed the dogs' howling as simply a mechanical response—as little different from the noise of a clock whose springs have been struck. Similarly, until the early 1980s, American doctors performed major surgery on infants without using painkillers or any anesthetic; the babies' cries were explained as mere instinctive reactions.[77] And because African slaves were thought to feel less pain than white people, it was easier to justify the brutal experience of slavery.

Because the experience of pain is subjective, it is easy to argue against the suffering of another. In other words, since we aren't inside another's body, we can only assume what they may be feeling—and if we have a vested interested in assuming that they are not in pain, it is all too easy to believe this to be true. Our assumptions stem from our beliefs, and the very belief systems that enable us to inflict suffering on others actively work to keep themselves alive. So it is no wonder that we don't err on the side of caution— or reason—when it comes to carnistic practices that cause animals pain. Consider, for instance, the common assumption that it is nothing more than instinct that drives lobsters to scramble to escape the pot in which they are being boiled alive. Though we have no reason to believe that they are not in pain, though it is only logical to assume they are fleeing scalding water because it hurts, and though instinct and sentience can and do coexist (one does not preclude the other), most people choose to believe otherwise.

Objective research is one way to counter our subjective perception of others' experience. Researchers have, for instance, demonstrated that neural pathways in neonates are developed enough for infants to feel pain, and neonates are no longer denied anesthetics. Scientists have also presented sufficient evidence that crustaceans are indeed sentient; some municipalities have therefore made it illegal to boil lobsters alive,[78] and Whole Foods Market, the world's leading organic and natural-food retailer, no longer sells live lobsters or soft-shell crabs on the grounds that their handling and sale is inhumane.[79]

And despite the poultry industry's claims that humans cannot truly know how chickens feel, there is now evidence that strongly suggests birds not only suffer, but actively seek to anesthetize their pain. Researchers took a group of 120 chickens, half of whom were lame, and offered them two types of feed: normal feed and feed that contained an anti-inflammatory painkiller. The lame chickens consumed up to 50 percent more drugged feed than did the nonlame birds and walked better as a result. A second, similar study found that the more severe a chicken's lameness, the more of the drugged feed the bird consumed. Researchers concluded that the birds were likely self-medicating and that they can, and do, suffer.[80]

EGGED ON AND ON: EGG-LAYING HENS

It is ironic that so many of our "cute" pictures of animals—on cards, in posts, in calendars, and so forth—contain images of newly born chicks, when every year millions of these baby birds are treated in ways that most of us wouldn't imagine. Egg-laying hens, or birds used for egg production, are born in commercial hatcheries, in industrial incubators. The male chicks are of no economic value and are therefore discarded shortly after birth. They can be dumped into a massive grinder and ground up alive, gassed, or thrown in garbage bins where they die from suffocation or dehydration.[81] About 80 percent of egg-laying factory-farmed hens are stuffed into battery cages, which are wire cages that hold an average of six birds and are about the size of a square filing cabinet.[82]

Hens spend their entire lives in battery cages,[83] where they must eat, sleep, and defecate; and where they cannot even open their wings. The bottoms of the cages are made of wire so that the bird's droppings can fall through the openings, and the hens' limbs can easily become entangled in the mesh. The wires on the sides and top of the cages scrape off the birds' feathers and cause bruises, and some hens neurotically rub their chests against these wires until they are bald and bleeding. Battery cages are considered so cruel that they have been banned in a number of countries and some states, though they remain widely used throughout the US.[84]

Because the hens have been genetically manipulated to lay twenty to thirty times as many eggs as their ancestors,[85] their brittle bones frequently break, as the calcium in their skeletons is disproportionately diverted to eggshell formation. Another consequence of this artificial selection to lay unnaturally large numbers of eggs is uterine prolapse. When an egg gets stuck against the uterine wall, it can pull the uterus out with it. Unless the uterus is pushed back into the hen's body, other hens will peck at it until she bleeds to death or dies of infection; in each case, it usually takes two days for the hen to die.[86]

When they can no longer produce eggs profitably, the hens are pulled out of their cages, sometimes several in a handful, and their limbs, which are weakened and ensnared in the wires, often tear. When she is just over one year old, the egg-laying hen is sent to slaughter.[87]

DEATH BY WOOD CHIPPER: HUMANE, OR INSANE?

In 2003, the LA Times reported that workers at an egg ranch in San Diego fed "squirming birds by the bucket into [a wood chipper], then turn[ed] the mashed remains with dirt and heap[ed] the mixture into piles." According to the Times, veterinarian Gregg Cutler, a member of the animal welfare committee of the American Veterinary Medical Association, authorized the procedure.[88] Prior to the incident, Cutler had been in attendance at a meeting of poultry ranchers discussing how to deal with chickens during an outbreak of Newcastle disease, an avian viral infection. Cutler told the Times that "[n]o idea was too crazy. We were in desperation trying to deal with this disease." But the 30,000 hens who were being tossed into the wood chipper in San Diego were not infected with Newcastle disease; they had simply stopped producing eggs. Still, according to one of the ranch owners, Cutler and other veterinarians approved the procedure and called it humane. Charges were not pressed against Cutler, and though the San Diego district attorney's office investigated the ranch to assess for animal cruelty, they concluded that there was no evidence of criminal intent on the part of the owners, who were "just following professional advice."

GOT MILK?
COWS RAISED FOR DAIRY

Because most people believe it is possible to procure milk without harming the cow, they assume that dairy products are naturally cruelty free. "Naturally" is the operative word here since, like all contemporary carnistic products, milk production is anything but natural.

Many cows in the United States spend their lives in dairy factories, where they are either chained by the neck and confined within tiny stalls in sheds, or live outdoors in overcrowded, fenced-in feedlots. In the feedlots, the cows eat out of a conveyor belt along a fence, and the ground they stand and lie on is concrete, saturated with urine and feces.[89]

Cows raised for dairy are injected with genetically engineered growth hormones and are artificially impregnated every year, in order to maximize milk production.[90] In most dairies in the United States, the cows are milked by machines for ten months of the year, which includes the nine-to-ten-month period during which they are pregnant.[91] This process of continual impregnation and lactation stresses their bodies so much that many cows develop lameness and mastitis, an infection and sometimes-massive inflammation of the udder. The cow's system is so overworked that her normal metabolic process may be insufficient to keep up with her physical output, and so her natural, herbivorous diet of grazing pasture is supplemented with grain and high-protein, carnivorous feedstuffs made of animal derivatives such as blood products, gelatin, and tallow.[92]

Though the physical stress these cows endure is significant, it is quite possible that their greatest suffering comes from the emotional trauma they endure each year after giving birth. Their male offspring are used to produce veal,[93] and the females are used for dairy production. As I mentioned earlier, cows are intimately bonded with their calves, whom they may nurse for up to a year. In dairy factories, however, the calf is removed usually within hours of birth so the cow's milk can be diverted for human consumption. Often the calf is dragged away from the mother, as the cow bellows hysterically. Other times, to prevent the cow from being provoked, she is taken to another part of the facility to be milked, and the calf is removed in her absence. Like human mothers, cows can become frenzied and desperate when they cannot find their offspring. They will bellow for days, frantically searching for their calves, and sometimes even turning violent., thrashing and kicking at workers. There are even instances of cows escaping and traveling for miles to find their calves on other farms.[94]

Though cows have a natural lifespan of approximately twenty years, after only four years in a dairy factory they are considered spent and are sent to slaughter.[95] A significant proportion of US ground beef is made from cows who had been used for dairy.[96]

OUT OF THE MOUTHS
OF BABES: VEAL

Many people have a soft spot for babies, bovines notwithstanding. Most of us are touched by the sight of a newborn calf entering the world, and sympathize with his or her innocence, fragility, and vulnerability. In fact, wobbly legged calves are often favorites of children's books. Imagine, then, the shock of many people when they learn of the plight of the approximately one million calves a year who are the unwanted by-products of the dairy industry. In fact, if it weren't for the dairy industry, the veal industry would likely not exist.[97]

Because the male calves who are born to cows used for dairy are of no use to dairy farmers, they are essentially disposed of. Days or even hours after birth, the calves are herded onto a truck—and some need to be dragged since they are not yet able to walk properly, a practice that is now considered inhumane by the USDA.[98] These calves end up at auctions, where they may be sold for as little as $50 to veal producers,[99] and since they are literally newborns, it is not unusual for calves in the auction ring to have hides still slick from the womb and the umbilical cord still dangling from their stomachs.[100]

For the duration of their short lives—though some are killed within days, most of these calves live for sixteen to eighteen weeks—they are chained or tethered at the neck and confined to stalls so tiny they can't even turn around or lie down normally.*[101] And in order to produce the pale color that veal is known for, the animals are typically fed an unnatural diet lacking in iron, so that they are in a state of chronic borderline anemia. Calves raised for veal spend their lives immobilized and sickly, and not surprisingly, they have been observed to exhibit some of the same neurotic behaviors as other animals under intense stress: abnormal head tossing and scraping, kicking, scratching, and chewing.

The slaughter of calves is no different than the slaughter of other animals; they are meant to be stunned before being shackled,[103] but again, this method is far from perfect. A worker that Eisnitz interviewed described a part of the process:

> In the morning the big holdup was the calves. To get done with them faster, we'd put eight or nine of them in the knocking box at a time. As soon as they start going in, you start shooting, the calves are jumping, they're all piling up on top of each other. You don't know which ones got shot and which ones didn't get shot at all, and you forget to do the bottom ones. They're hung anyway, and down the line they go, wriggling and yelling. The baby ones—two, three weeks old—I felt bad killing them so I just let them walk past.[104]

---

* Veal crates are banned in some US states and in the EU[102].

There seems to be a point at which the violence of carnism is such that even the most powerful defenses of the system will falter.

SEA FOOD, OR SEA LIFE?
FISH AND OTHER AQUATIC ANIMALS

Many of us feel so removed from fish and other commonly consumed animals from the sea* that we don't even think of their flesh as meat. For instance, when a meat eater** learns that someone is vegetarian, the meat eater will often respond by asking, "So, you only eat fish?" We tend not to perceive aquatic animals' flesh as meat because—though we know they're neither plants nor minerals—we often don't think of aquatic animals *as* animals. And by extension, we don't think of these beings as sentient, as having lives that matter to them. We thus relate to the animals of the sea as if they were anomalous plants, plucking them from the ocean as easily as we pluck an apple from a tree.

But are aquatic animals the mindless, insensate organisms many of us assume them to be? Not according to a number of neurobiologists, animal behaviorists, and other scientists around the world. There is a significant body of research demonstrating that fish and other animals from the sea possess both intelligence and the capacity to feel pain. Research on the intelligence of aquatic animals has, for example, yielded evidence that fish do not forget what they've experienced just moments before, but have a memory span of at least three months.[105] Moreover, Oxford University scientist

---

* Aquatic animals come from both salt- and freshwater bodies. However, at times I use the term "sea" in reference to aquatic animals because the vast majority of aquatic animals come from the ocean, and because I wish to avoid cumbersome language.
** As I mentioned in chapter 2, "meat eater" does not accurately represent the phenomenon of carnistic consumption. A more appropriate phrase would be "carnistic consumer." However, so as not to bog the reader down with too much unfamiliar terminology, I have chosen to use "meat eater" throughout this book.

Dr. Theresa Burt de Perera determined that fish can develop "mental maps" of their surroundings that allow them to memorize and navigate changes in their environment—a task that is beyond the cognitive ability of hamsters. Because of such findings, it is now illegal in the city of Monza, Italy, to keep goldfish confined in small bowls.[106] And lobsters, some of whom have a lifespan longer than that of humans, possess over 400 types of chemical receptors on their antennae, which, according to Dr. Jelle Atema of the Marine Biological Laboratory in Woods Hole, Massachusetts, may enable them to detect the sex, species, and even mood of another animal.

I pointed out earlier in this chapter that scientists have demonstrated the sentience of some types of crustaceans such that legislation has been passed protecting these species. Similarly, evidence that other aquatic animals can feel pain is amassing; for instance, researchers have found that fish have a number of pain receptors in various parts of their bodies, and they emit neurotransmitters that act as pain killers much as human endorphins do.[107] In one study, researchers from the Roslin Institute and the University of Edinburgh injected the lips of one group of fish with a painful, acidic substance and they injected the lips of another group with saline. The first group of fish exhibited a rocking motion "strikingly similar to the kind of motion seen in stressed . . . mammals." Moreover, the animals were clearly suffering: they rubbed their lips on the gravel in their tank and against the tank walls, and didn't resume feeding for almost three times longer than the control group. (This study has spurred the debate about the ethics of recreational fishing, with animal advocates arguing that impaling fish in their mouths for fun is a form of animal cruelty.)

Other research has suggested that aquatic animals may actually experience a post-traumatic reaction to pain. In a landmark study, scientists from Purdue University and the

Norwegian School of Veterinary Science attached foil heaters to two groups of fish, and administered morphine to one group. They raised the temperature of the foil to observe the reaction of the fish (no fish were permanently harmed in the experiment). The researchers assumed that the morphine would enable the fish to withstand more heat. As it turned out, both groups of fish wriggled at the same temperature, leading the researchers to conclude that the wriggling was a reflexive reaction and didn't indicate pain. However, after the fish had been returned to their tanks, those who hadn't been given morphine exhibited defensive behaviors, indicating anxiety or wariness. The researchers determined that the fish were having a post-traumatic response to the pain: "They turned that pain into fear like we do."

Nevertheless, in the United States, 47 billion aquatic animals are slaughtered each year, many of whom are destined for human consumption.[108] There are two ways that these animals are captured, raised, and killed: by commercial fishing and through aquatic farming.[109] Each of these methods causes intensive suffering to the animals and extensive damage to the environment.

Commercial fishing is responsible not only for the depletion of 90 percent of the world's fish stocks, or subpopulations,[110] but also for serious injury to other species of animals. One method used to catch fish is by dragging long nets beneath the surface of the ocean. These nets result in massive amounts of "bycatch"—captured animals other than those targeted.[111] It is estimated that each year, over 63 million pounds, or 30 million tons, of sea animals, including birds, turtles, dolphins, and unwanted fish, are thrown back into the ocean, dead or dying; and nets left at sea continue to ensnare seabirds and other animals who unwittingly encounter them.[112] In some places, fisheries use dynamite or cyanide in lieu of nets, but such methods can destroy entire ecosystems.[113] Commercial fishing poses such a threat to marine biodiversity that it's been referred to as "underwater clear-cutting."

Some people choose to eat farm-raised fish rather than commercially caught fish to help preserve the oceans' biodiversity. However, most of the feed used for farm-raised fish comes from the sea; it is estimated that for every pound of farmed salmon (the third-most-consumed fish in the US) produced, up to five pounds of marine life are used. Farmed fish are raised in aquafarms, which are CAFOs for sea animals and which produce 21 percent of the fish consumed in the US and 47 percent of the fish consumed globally.[114] These facilities can be either land based, in controlled, indoor environments; or ocean based, situated close to the shoreline. Both types of aquafarms hold tens of thousands of fish or other aquatic animals packed into overcrowded pens that are rife with parasites and disease. To control for illness, accelerate growth, and modify reproductive behaviors, the animals are given antibiotics, pesticides, and hormones and some are genetically modified.[115] The chemicals are absorbed by the animals and also leech out into the environment, ending up in our digestive systems and our ecosystem. It is not uncommon for fish to escape from ocean-based pens, and when they do, they may spread disease or reproduce and contaminate the gene pool.[116]

Fish may be slaughtered in a number of ways.[117] Commercially caught fish are often left to suffocate to death after being landed. Farmed fish are typically removed from their pens by a pump, and dumped into a slaughter area. There, various slaughter methods may be applied, including electrocution, which leads to a lethal, epileptic-like seizure; percussive stunning, which is administering a blow to the head with a club; live chilling, in which the animal is left on ice and frozen alive; suffocation; or spiking, where a spike is inserted through the animal's brain.

Despite the violence inherent in the production of sea food, many people are undisturbed by the sight of at least some aspects of this process. So the primary defense of the carnistic system, invisibility, plays a lesser role when it comes to processing aquatic animals; most people can witness fish slaughter, for instance, without experiencing the trauma they might feel witnessing the slaughter of a pig. It would seem that, because aquatic animals appear so fundamentally different from humans, so alien, we feel sufficiently distanced from them so that their suffering remains invisible even when it's in plain sight.

COMPASSIONATE CARNISM: "HUMANE" MEAT, EGGS, AND DAIRY

In recent years, as awareness of the violence inherent in contemporary animal agriculture has risen, more and more people have chosen to withhold their support from an industry that they recognize runs counter to their core moral values of compassion and justice. So of course, carnistic industry has sought to counter this trend, in no small part by offering people the option of consuming animals who are supposedly happy to be eaten—by producing so-called humane meat, eggs, and dairy.

"Humanely" raised animals often suffer extensively. Even though they have more room to move around, they are often nevertheless still subjected to painful practices, such as castration without anesthesia (as with meat production) or having their offspring thrown into meat grinders (as with egg production) or removed hours after birth (as with dairy production). And almost all animals ultimately end up at essentially the same slaughterhouses.[118] As such, the very notion of humane carnistic products is irrational.

It can be difficult to appreciate the absurdity of "compassionate carnism" unless we step outside the carnistic box. So consider this: most of us would find it cruel to slaughter a happy, healthy, golden retriever simply because people like the way her thighs taste—yet when the exact same thing is done to individuals of other species, we are expected to consider it humane. Humane meat, eggs, and dairy—compassionate carnism—is, indeed, a contradiction in terms.

"THIS OBSCENE . . . TORTURE HAS GOT TO STOP, AND ONLY PEOPLE LIKE US CAN HELP."

In South Korea, millions of dogs are killed for their meat every year. While the Korean dogmeat trade is not officially sanctioned by the government, neither is it reprehended.

In 2002, the British *Telegraph* published an article documenting the lives and deaths of the dogs raised for their meat:

> The stench and the yelps of caged dogs may be stomach churning, but Lee Wha-jin happily slaps down dishes of dog-meat stew on the white plastic tabletops of his restaurant in the notorious Moran night market in Seoul.
>
> At the rear of shop after shop, eight-month-old puppies—considered to be the prime age for eating—are packed into tiny cages welded together in rows three or four high.
>
> Customers choose which of the live animals they want. The dog is then taken to the back of the shop where a flimsy curtain or a swinging door obscures the sight, but not the sound, of a hideous death. . . .

Before arriving in the grim array of cages behind restaurants, most dogs have had to endure the misery of a Korean canine farm hidden in the hills of the countryside. It is not unusual for puppies to grow up 10 to a cage, covered in sores and lice. . . .

The dogs' deaths are as inhumane as their rearing. The majority are beaten to death, as it is thought to stimulate the production of adrenalin that South Korean men believe will bolster their virility.

Once dead, or nearly dead, the dogs are dropped into boiling water, skinned and hung by the jaw from a meat hook. Many cooks then use a blow torch to glaze the carcass.[119]

The South Korean dogmeat trade has been met with violent opposition from animal advocacy groups and foreigners—many of whom regularly consume the meat of pigs, chickens, and bovines. Lee Won-Bok, president of the Korea Association for Animal Protection, said, "It's horrible to imagine dog meat on display next to beef and ham at supermarkets." And horrified bloggers on the American Society for the Prevention of Cruelty to Animals (ASPCA)'s website echoed his sentiment. Like Won-Bok, the bloggers have given voice to what many people feel when they become aware of animal cruelty:*

[D]ecent people can not bring themselves to confront this issue because of the sheer and utter horror food and fur dogs/cats etc. go through in

---

* The following statements are not my own; they are from online commenters who no doubt consume meat from cows, chickens, and pigs but nevertheless decry the production and consumption of meat from dogs. These comments are simply intended to highlight the fact that consumers of carnistic products typically fail to see the contradiction in their own beliefs and behaviors.

the far east, millions of dogs and cats are skinned alive, boiled alive, some even skinned alive THEN boiled alive. [T]he far east is responsible for the worst, most obscene cruelty towards animals this planet has ever seen, and it's on a vast scale.

. . . [M]ost people only see and hear what they want to and that because this isn't taking place here in the USA that people will tend to ignore it but just because this is happening overseas it won't go away. People need to get their heads out of the sand and stand up for these animals.

For dogs that are eventually killed for consumption, if they even have a life, it is a life of sheer misery. . . . Dogs are neither wild animals nor live-stock. . . . Everyone all over the world must act now. Save dogs in Korea. We believe you can.

[I']ve seen cruelty from all around the world, but the far east is truly shocking in its attitude towards animals why is this? [M]y theory is cos [sic] they know the enlightened west generally give dogs/cats the respect they deserve, and their backward societys [sic] are unwilling to catch up.

[I] gather that many [people] are utterly ignorant of the situation in the Far East, and to be honest you can not really blame them, after all, how many decent people would even dream that animals could be subjected to such unnecessary alien cruelty.

[D]ecent people everywhere have to confront this issue, despite the fact it will give them nightmares. . . .

[T]his obscene satanic devlish [sic] torture has got to stop, and only people like us can help.

IF SLAUGHTERHOUSES
HAD GLASS WALLS

Sir Paul McCartney once claimed that if slaughterhouses had glass walls, everyone would be vegetarian. He believed that if we knew the truth about meat production, we'd be unable to continue eating animals.

Yet on some level we do know the truth. We know that carnistic production is a messy business, but we choose not to know just how messy it is. We know that meat comes from animals, but we choose not to connect the dots. And often, we eat animals and choose not to know we're even making a choice. Violent ideologies are structured so that it is not only possible, but inevitable, that we are aware of an unpleasant truth on one level while being oblivious to it on another. Common to all violent ideologies is this phenomenon of *knowing without knowing.* And it is the essence of carnism.

Inherent in violent ideologies is an implicit contract between producer and consumer to see no evil, hear no evil, and speak no evil. Sure, carnistic businesses go to great lengths to protect their secrets. But we make their job easy for them. They tell us not to look, and we turn away. They tell us the billions of animals who we never see live outdoors on peaceful farms, and as illogical as this is, we don't question it. We make their job easy because on some level most of us don't want to know the way things really are.

But at the same time, we also want and deserve the freedom to make informed decisions, to be free thinkers and active consumers. Such freedom is obviously impossible if we aren't even aware that we are making choices in the first place. When an invisible ideology guides our beliefs and behaviors, we become casualties of a system that has stolen our freedom to think for ourselves and to act accordingly.

When we understand the way things really are—when we recognize the inner workings of the system—then, and only then, are we in a position to make our choices freely. Naming carnism and demystifying the practices of carnistic production can help us begin to see through the façade of the system. Schlosser eloquently expresses this point, and it seems only fitting to end this chapter with the conclusion of his journey through the lives and deaths of the animals we eat:

> As I walk along the fence, a group of cattle approaches me, looking me straight in the eye, like dogs hoping for a treat, and follow me, out of some mysterious impulse. I stop and try to absorb the whole scene: the cool breeze, the cattle and their gentle lowing, a cloudless sky, steam rising from the [meat] plant in the moonlight. And then I notice that the building does have one window, a small square of light on the second floor. It offers a glimpse of what's hidden behind this huge, blank façade. Through the little window you can see bright-red carcasses on hooks, going round and round.[120]

CHAPTER 4

Collateral Damage: The Other Casualties of Carnism

Facts do not cease to exist because they are ignored.
—ALDOUS HUXLEY

In chapter 3 we explored the lives and deaths of the animals most commonly raised for meat, eggs, and dairy products in the United States. For the sake of brevity, I did not discuss the less-frequently consumed animals, such as lambs, goats, and ducks. I also didn't mention an important group of animals who are the other casualties of carnism, animals who are the all-too-often-overlooked *collateral damage* of animal agribusiness.

Like pigs and other species we have discussed, the vast majority of these animals—over 300 million of them—are treated as commodities, as means to ends. Like the other animals, their welfare impedes profit. And like the other animals, they are offered little protection by the law.

These other casualties of carnism are rarely the focus of attention when discussing carnistic production. They, too, are invisible victims— not because they are not seen, but because they are not recognized. They are the human animals. They are the factory workers, the residents who live near polluting CAFOs, the carnistic consumers, the taxpayers. They are you and me. *We* are the collateral damage of carnism; we pay for carnism with our health, our environment, and our taxes—$13.2 billion a year (in farm subsidies), to be exact.[121]*

Workers in meatpacking plants** spend virtually all of their waking hours in crowded factories with floors that may be covered in blood and grease.[124] The relentless pace of the disassembly line keeps them at constant risk of serious injury or even death.[125] And CAFO employees—who are exposed to noxious gases from concentrated wastes—may develop serious respiratory disease, reproductive dysfunction, neurological degeneration, and seizures; and they may even fall into comas.[126]

Such congested and dangerous working conditions can lead to a variety of other physical maladies,[127] but these employees rarely receive medical treatment since it is more cost effective to lose some of them prematurely than to attend to their physical needs. Not surprisingly, like other animals who must be prodded along when they resist following orders, workers in animal factories may be bullied, both physically and psychologically, if they fail to respond to demands.[128]

Residents who live near CAFOs have been poisoned by factory wastes, including sulfites and nitrates. These toxins contaminate the air and drinking water and can lead to chronic asthma and eye irritation, bronchitis, diarrhea, severe headaches, nausea, spontaneous abortions, birth defects, infant death, and viral and bacterial disease outbreaks.[129]

And meat, egg, and dairy consumers—over 317 million Americans—are unknowingly fed an array of contaminants. Carnistic foods are often laced with synthetic hormones, some of which have been linked to the development of various cancers and are banned from both human and animal

---

* Although carnistic producers do not receive direct financial support under the 2014 Farm Bill (nor did they under the pre-2014 program), they are nevertheless eligible for emergency and disaster relief, which cost $9.8 billion between 1995 and 2016.[122] Similarly, in the EU, subsidies of approximately €30 billion go to carnistic producers, representing about 19 percent of the block's total annual budget.[123]

** Conditions in dairy and egg production facilities are similar to those in meatpacking plants.

consumption in the European Union;[130] massive doses of antibiotics; toxic pesticides, herbicides, and fungicides that are known carcinogens; potentially deadly strains of bacteria and viruses; petroleum; poisoned rat carcasses; dirt; hair; and feces.[131]

In *Fast Food Nation*, Eric Schlosser captures the essence of the collateral damage of carnism: "There's shit in the meat." Yet while Schlosser was referring specifically to fecal matter, the subject of this chapter includes far more than just feces. It's everything that contaminates the meat, eggs, and dairy we eat, from corruption to disease. It is the refuse of a sick system.

The story of how shit got in our meat is the story of one of the central characteristics of carnism, and of other violent ideologies: the system depends on a constituency of *indirect* victims, inadvertent victims who not only suffer the consequences of the system, but who also help that system by unwittingly participating in their own victimization. The system creates such victims by appearing to be something it is not, so that we feel safe when we are at risk and free when we have been coerced. The story of how shit got in our meat is the story of the human casualties of carnism.

HOW SAFE ARE WE?

In 1906, Upton Sinclair published *The Jungle*, his famous exposé on the meatpacking industry. *The Jungle* documented the corruption of animal agribusinesses and the filthy, dangerous conditions that characterized meatpacking plants and slaughterhouses. Sinclair described factories where workers stood in half an inch of blood, on killing floors teeming with rats—living and dead—some of whom ended up processed along with the meat. The workers were at constant risk of getting their fingers sliced off and of falling into vats of lard, "overlooked for days, till all but the bones of them had gone out to the world as Durham's Pure Leaf Lard!"[132] *The Jungle* exposed conditions so appalling and disgusting that the public and policymakers alike were outraged. Such widespread indignation led to the passage of the Meat Inspection Act and the Pure Food and Drug Act, which mandated regular inspections of slaughterhouses and meatpacking plants.

Many people have heard of *The Jungle* and its impact on laws regulating meat production. However, few realize that these laws were rarely enforced, and that the decades following the publication of *The Jungle* saw little improvement in factory conditions. In fact, in many ways, today conditions are even worse; the advent of larger plants and faster processing technologies, coupled with inadequate numbers of federal inspectors, have made workers more burdened and facilities even more crowded and difficult to police.

INFECTIONS, INSPECTIONS, AND THE USDA

Inspections take place on two levels: up close and from a distance. In accordance with the Meat Inspection Act of 1906, USDA inspectors were to perform up-close inspections: they were to check animals' organs and other body parts for disease, equipment for microbes, carcasses for early signs of contamination and insects, and walls and rooms for proper sanitation. However, in the 1980s, new legislation shifted the burden of quality control from the government to the plants themselves[133] (and recently, the Trump administration further aggravated the situation by nearly halving the number of federal inspectors required at a given plant).[134] This means that the corporations' own employees, rather than federal inspectors, are now primarily responsible for the closer inspections—employees who receive virtually no formal training and can't identify many of the signs of contamination and disease, and who often don't speak English well enough to communicate what they do find.[135] Since the passing of the new legislation, studies in several plants revealed that corporate inspectors didn't know that a piece of meat that had a USDA tag on it was condemned, and they couldn't recognize the signs of measles.[136] These investigations also revealed that corporate inspectors were unable to recognize infections unless there was pus oozing out of an abscess. In fact, it appears that in our nation's meatpacking plants, contaminated meat is the rule, rather than the exception. A recent study in which retail meat samples were tested for E. coli revealed that 76.7 percent of ground turkey, 63.4 percent of chicken, 47.3 percent of ground beef, and 33.8 percent of pork chops were contaminated;[137] and according to a study published in the *Journal of Food Protection* fecal contamination was found in 85 percent of fish filets procured from retail markets and the Internet.[138] What's more, the World Health Organization has warned that avian influenza—the potentially deadly virus sometimes referred to as "bird flu"—may be spread through the fecal matter of infected birds.[139]

Even if workers were able to identify contaminated body parts, food quality standards are so low that many defective carcasses would still pass inspection.[140] Consider the joint investigation by the *Guardian* and the Bureau of Investigative Journalism (TBIJ) of unpublished US government records, which revealed a number of incidents, such as "pig carcasses piling up on the factory floor after an equipment breakdown, leading to contamination with grease, blood, and other filth; meat destined for human [consumption] found riddled with fecal matter and abscesses filled with pus . . . factory floors flooded with dirty water after drains became blocked by meat parts and other debris; [and] dirty chicken, soiled with feces or having been dropped on the floor being put back on the production line after being rinsed with diluted chlorine."[141] And in 2007, the *Chicago Tribune* ran an article exposing how the USDA deemed it acceptable for animal agribusinesses to sell meat that's been contaminated with E. coli, as long as the meat was labeled "cook only," for use in precooked meat products (including those that ended up in school lunches).[142]

Unhygienic conditions of the buildings and machinery may also pose a threat to human health.[143] The aforementioned joint *Guardian*-TBIJ report revealed that "diseased meat—condemned from entering the human food chain—was placed in a container meant for edible product; meat soiled with faecal matter was also recorded, with an inspector noting '. . . I observed a poultry intestine in the liver bin. The intestine was approximately 6.5 inches long and had visible faeces oozing out both ends;' a pig's head was found to have partially covered a drain, leading to 'bloody waste water filling the area'; inspectors found a stainless steel hand-wash sink 'plugged and approximately one-quarter full of standing bloody water with pieces of fat and meat.' Production employees use this sink to clean and sanitise their hands and gloves. . . ."

Some USDA inspectors have expressed grave concern about the unhygienic conditions in meatpacking plants, and yet they have little voice to enact change.[144] The vast inadequacies of the current inspection system were described in another 2007 *Chicago Tribune* article. Felicia Nestor, a senior policy analyst for Food and Water Watch, a Washington, DC–based food safety group, told the *Tribune*: "Inspectors are not . . . in the vast majority of processing plants full time. For the most part, inspectors at processing plants are on patrols, meaning they cover a number of plants."[145] And federal officers reported that inspection goals haven't been met for years; their workload is so overwhelming that they perform mere cursory checks of company records, rather than conduct physical examinations of the meat. Inspectors spend their time monitoring a meat company's hazard-analysis plan and have no time to actually enforce the USDA's inspection regulations. One inspector told the *Tribune*, "They [meatpacking companies] write their own plan. They write everything for themselves. We're 'monitoring' that now. It's just a joke. We mostly check paper now. You can put anything you want on paper."

What this all comes down to is that corporations, whose primary objective is to increase their profit margin, are left to police themselves. We have left the fox to guard the chicken coop. And not surprisingly, we have ended up with shit in our meat.

THE HUMAN SLAUGHTERHOUSE ANIMAL

Meat has long stood for the freedom to exploit freely.
—NICK FIDDES, *Meat: A Natural Symbol*

Many workers in US meatpacking plants are undocumented immigrants from Central and South America and Asia who receive little, if any, training.[146] Schlosser interviewed a bleeder (slaughterhouse worker) who told him, "Nobody helped train me—no training how to use the knife. . . . So you see how the people on either side of you do the work, and then you do it."[147] Besides having to perform jobs for which they are wholly unprepared, these employees find themselves in working conditions that are exploitative, hazardous, unsanitary, and violent. They spend hour upon hour in a death-saturated, high-stress environment, and they suffer for it—imagine making one knife cut every two or three seconds, totaling approximately *10,000* cuts a day.[148] In an interview with *Mother Jones* magazine, Schlosser commented on the relentless pace of the production line:

The golden rule in meatpacking plants is "The Chain Will Not Stop." . . . Nothing stands in the way of production, not mechanical failures, breakdowns, accidents. Forklifts crash, saws overheat, workers drop knives, workers get cut, workers collapse and lie unconscious on the floor, as dripping carcasses sway past them, and the chain keeps going . . . a . . . worker told me, "I've seen bleeders, and they're gushing because they got hit right in the vein, and I mean they're almost passing out, and here comes the supply guy again, with the bleach, to clean the blood off the floor, but the chain never stops. It never stops."[149]

Not surprisingly, meatpacking is arguably the most dangerous factory job in the United States,[150] and it is undoubtedly the most violent. For instance, workers must wear hockey masks to prevent their teeth from getting kicked out by conscious animals being dragged along a conveyor belt.[151] And consider the titles of accident reports issued by the federal Occupational Safety and Health Administration (OSHA), which provide snapshots of the perilous conditions: *Employee Hospitalized for Neck Laceration from Flying Blade. Employee's Eye Injured When Struck by Hanging Hook. Employee's Arm Amputated When Caught in Meat Tenderizer. Employee Decapitated by Chain of Hide Puller Machine. Employee Killed When Head Crushed in Hide Fleshing Machine. Caught and Killed by Gut-Cooker Machine.*[152] In fact, in 2005, for the first time ever, Human Rights Watch issued a report criticizing a single US industry—the meat industry—for working conditions so appalling they violate basic human rights.[153]

OPERATIONAL HAZARDS IN THE MEATPACKING INDUSTRY

Operation Performed	Equipment/ Substances	Accidents/ Injuries
Stunning	Knocking gun	Severe shock, body punctures
Skinning/ removing front legs	Pincher device	Amputations, eye injuries, cuts, falls
Splitting animal	Splitter saws	Eye injuries, carpal tunnel syndrome, amputations, cuts, falls
Removing brain	Head splitter	Cuts, amputations, eye injuries, falls
Transporting products	Screw conveyers, screw auger	Fractures, cuts, amputations, falls
Cutting/ trimming/boning	Hand knives, saws, circular saw, band saw	Cuts, eye injuries, carpal tunnel syndrome, falls
Removing jaw bone/snout	Jaw bone/ snout puller	Amputations, falls
Preparing bacon for slicing	Bacon/belly press	Amputations, falls
Tenderizing	Electrical meat tenderizers	Severe shock, amputations, cuts, eye injuries
Cleaning equipment	Lock-out, tag-out	Amputations, cuts
Hoisting/ shackling	Chain/dolly assembly	Falls, falling carcasses

Wrapping meat	Sealant machine/ polyvinyl chloride, meat	Exposure to toxic substances, severe burns to hands and arms, falls
Lugging meat	Carcasses	Severe back and shoulder injuries, falls
Refrigeration/ curing, cleaning, wrapping	Ammonia, carbon dioxide, carbon monoxide, polyvinyl chloride	Upper respiratory irritation and damage

Source: Publication of the US Department of Labor, Occupational and Safety Health Administration (OSHA)

CONDITIONED KILLERS

Given the brutality of the carnistic process, it's easy to assume that the people whose job it is to kill animals are sadistic or otherwise psychologically disturbed. Yet while psychological disturbance and even sadism may *result* from prolonged exposure to violence, they do not necessarily *cause* individuals to seek out a career in killing. In any violent ideology, those in the business of killing may not be jaded when they start out, but they eventually grow accustomed to violence that once disturbed them. Such acclimation reflects the defense mechanism *routinization*— routinely performing an action until one becomes desensitized, or numbed, to it. For instance, agricultural investigator Gail Eisnitz interviewed a slaughterhouse worker who told her:

> The worst thing, worse than the physical danger, is the emotional toll. If you work in that stick pit for any period of time, you develop an attitude that lets you kill things but doesn't let you care. You may look a hog in the eye that's walking around down in the blood pit with you and think, "God, that really isn't a bad-looking animal." You may want to pet it. Pigs

down on the kill floor have come up and nuzzled me like a puppy. Two minutes later, I had to kill them—beat them to death with a pipe. I can't care.[154]

And the more desensitized workers become—the more they "can't care"—the greater the buildup of their psychological distress. Most people can experience only so much violence before they become traumatized by it; studies of combat veterans, for instance, demonstrate again and again the profound effect exposure to violence has on the psyche, particularly when one has also been a participant in that violence.[155] Traumatized workers become increasingly violent toward both animals and humans, and may develop addictive behaviors in an attempt to numb their distress. The worker Eisnitz interviewed described how he'd "had ideas of hanging [the] foreman upside down on the line and sticking him."[156] This worker went on to explain:

> Most stickers have been arrested for assault. A lot of them have problems with alcohol. They have to drink, they have no other way of dealing with killing live, kicking animals all day long. . . . A lot of guys . . . just drink and drug their problems away. Some of them end up abusing their spouses because they can't get rid of the feelings. They leave work with this attitude and they go down to the bar to forget. Only problem is, even if you try to drink those feelings away, they're still there when you sober up.[157]

Another worker told Eisnitz:

> I've taken out my job pressure and frustration on the animals. [T]here was a live hog in the pit. It hadn't done anything wrong, wasn't even running around the pit. It was just alive. I took a three-foot chunk of pipe—and I literally beat that hog to death.

Couldn't have been a two-inch piece of solid bone left in its head. Basically, if you want to put it in layman's terms, I crushed his skull. It was like I started hitting the hog and I couldn't stop. And when I finally did stop, I'd expended all this energy and frustration, and I'm thinking, what in God's sweet name did I do?[158]

And an undercover video shot by People for the Ethical Treatment of Animals revealed workers slamming piglets onto the floor, bragging about stabbing rods into sows' hind-quarters, and hitting pigs with metal rods. As one worker hits a sow with a metal rod, he yells, "I hate them. These (exple-tives) deserve to be hurt. Hurt, I say! Hurt! Hurt! Hurt! Hurt! . . . Take out your frustrations on 'em."[159]

Though the behavior of meatpackers may seem extreme and irrational, it is the inevitable result of working on the front lines of an extreme and irrational system.* Traumatized workers who, in turn, traumatize others are yet another casu-alty of the violent ideology that is carnism. Violence does indeed beget violence.

THE UNTOUCHABLES

Most people, whether they eat animals or not, share the same attitude toward the slaughter pro-cess: they see it as disgusting and offensive. Just as a type of meat that one finds disgusting tends to ren-der the foods it touches disgusting as well (would you continue eating a stew you'd picked dog meat out of?), so, too, does the process of slaughter seem to contaminate those who butcher animals.[160]

---

* Some slaughterhouse workers no doubt enter the industry as sociopaths—individuals who are antisocial, clinically "conscienceless," and often take pleasure in causing others to suffer. However, one must wonder at an industry that tolerates—indeed, *requires*—antisocial behaviors such as extreme aggression, remorselessness, and violence.

In various cultures and throughout history, professional butchers have been seen as impure, as taking on the immorality of killing animals and thereby protecting others from moral contamination. Often a group will have a designated individual or individuals who perform the butchering, and these people either will be "morally cleansed" before coming into contact with the others, or will live separately from the rest of the community. For instance, the designated butcher of the Bemba of Northern Rhodesia performs purification ceremonies after butchering, and the butchers of the ancient Guanches of the Canary Islands weren't allowed to enter others' homes or associate with those who weren't also butchers. In some cases, an entire social group is assigned the task of butchering: in Japan, for instance, butchers have been members of the Eta, an underclass whose members have been prevented from having contact with others; in India the Untouchables have been considered spiritually inferior and so have been relegated to spiritually "polluting" tasks such as butchering and working with leather; and in Tibet, professional butchers have been members of the lowest classes, because they violate the Buddhist tenet against killing.[161]

OUR PLANET, OUR SELVES

Even if you don't work in carnistic industry or eat animals, you are not immune to the consequences of the practices of the animal agribusinesses with which you share the planet. Carnistic production is a leading cause of every significant form of environmental damage: air and water pollution, biodiversity loss, erosion, deforestation, greenhouse gas emissions, and depletion of fresh water.[162]

In the industrialized world, the most immediate environmental consequence of carnistic production is the pollution caused by CAFOs.[163] Mounds of chemical- and disease-ridden waste produced by these factories leach into the ground and waterways and evaporate into the air, toxifying the environment and sicking the humans who reside nearby. CAFO runoff has been linked with a number of maladies, including respiratory problems, severe headaches, and digestive disorders. CAFO waste has also been connected with spontaneous abortions, birth defects, infant death, and disease outbreaks. In fact, CAFOs pose such a hazard to human health that the US department of Public Health has urged a moratorium on their toxic dumping.[164]

Yet animal agribusinesses have continued their practices unremittingly—because they can. Even though they are systematically destroying the environment and the people in it, animal agribusinesses aren't necessarily breaking any laws. How is it that the legal system, which was established to protect us from exploitation, ends up instead protecting the very industries that exploit us? Whatever happened to democracy?

THE ENVIRONMENTAL COSTS OF CARNISM[165]

- In 2006, the United Nations declared the livestock sector "one of the top two or three most significant contributors to the most serious environmental problems, at every scale from local to global." The UN warned, "The impact is so significant that it needs to be addressed with urgency."[166]

- In 2019, an international commission of 11,000 scientists proclaimed that people around the world must shift to a plant-focused (largely vegan) diet in order to help avert a global environmental catastrophe.[167]

- Animal agriculture is one of the top three contributors to water pollution. The main sources of the pollution are antibiotics and hormones, chemicals from tanneries, animal wastes, sediments from eroded pastures, and fertilizers and pesticides used for feed crops.[168]

- Over 75 percent of previously forested land in the Amazon has been converted into pastures for feeding farmed animals.[169]

- Thirty-seven percent of all pesticides and 50 percent of all antibiotics used in the US are used by animal agribusinesses.[170]

- Farmed animals must consume 2,000 pounds of grain in order to produce enough carnistic products to feed a person for a year. However, if that person ate the grains directly, it would take only 400 pounds of grain to feed them for a year.[171]

- Animal agriculture is responsible for more annual CO_2 emissions than that produced by 400 million cars.[172]

DEMOCRACY OR MEATOCRACY?

Bureaucracy helps render genocide unreal.
It . . . diminishes the emotional and intellectual tones
associated with the killing. . . . There is only a flow of
events to which most people . . . come to say yes. . . .
Mass murder is everywhere but at the same time nowhere.
—ROBERT JAY LIFTON, **The Nazi Doctors**

Violent ideologies speak their own language; core concepts are translated to maintain the system while appearing to support the people. Under carnism, for instance, democracy has become defined as having the freedom to choose among products that sicken our bodies and pollute our planet, rather than the freedom to eat our food and breathe our air without the risk of being poisoned. But violent ideologies are inherently undemocratic, as they rely on deception, secrecy, concentrated power, and coercion—all practices that are incompatible with a free society. While the larger system, or nation, may appear democratic, the violent system within it is not. This is one reason we don't recognize violent ideologies that exist within seemingly democratic systems; we simply aren't thinking to look for them.

In a democratic society, a central role of government is to create and implement policies and legislation that are in the best interest of its constituents. We therefore assume that the food that makes it to our plates isn't going to sicken or kill us. We assume this because we believe that those in our government work for us, the people who pay their salary; we assume the democratic process buffers us from those who might harm us.

However, when power is sufficiently concentrated within an industry, democracy becomes corrupted. Such is the case with carnism. US animal agribusiness is a $195 billion industry controlled by just a handful of corporations. These corporations are so powerful because they have become increasingly consolidated,[173] buying out all related businesses, including agro-chemical and seed companies, which produce pesticides, fertilizers, seeds, and other products; processing companies that buy and process animals; food manufacturers that process the meat, eggs, or dairy into specific products such as frozen entrees; food retailers, including supermarkets and restaurant chains; transportation systems, including railroads and shipping lines; pharmaceuticals; farm equipment such as tractors and irrigators; and even financial management plans. Economists warn that when any industry has a concentration ratio that runs upward of four companies controlling over 40 percent of the market (called CR4), competitiveness declines and serious issues, notably in the area of consumer protection, arise; the conglomerates are able to set prices and determine, for instance, food quality. Carnistic industry far exceeds CR4; for example, four beef packing companies control *83.5 percent* of the beef market. The power of animal agribusiness is such that the industry has become intertwined with government, blurring the boundary between private interests and public service.[174]

One process that has enabled the intertwining of the public and private sectors is the "revolving door" through which corporate executives and governmental officers exchange positions and strengthen networks. For instance, in 2004 both the current and former heads of the Grain Inspection, Packers and Stockyards Administration (GIPSA)—a division of the USDA that facilitates the marketing of livestock and other agricultural products—had worked with trade groups in the meatpacking industry.[175] And the then–USDA secretary Ann Veneman and other high-ranking officials had close former connections to agribusiness, especially in those industries they were supposed to oversee: Dale Moore, Veneman's chief of staff, was executive director for legislative affairs of the trade association National Cattlemen's Beef Association (NCBA); James Moseley, deputy secretary, co-owned a CAFO; and Mary Waters, assistant secretary for congressional relations, was legislative counsel and senior director for ConAgra, one of the nation's leading meat corporations.[176] And the process of the revolving door has not changed: in 2017, Craig Morris—who served as the deputy administrator of the Livestock, Poultry and Seed Program of the Agricultural Marketing Service at the USDA for thirteen years—became the vice president of international marketing for the National Pork Board.[177] Also in 2017, after nearly forty years working for the USDA Food Safety and Inspection Service, Alfred "Al" Almanza was appointed to the role of Global Head of Food Safety and Quality Assurance for JBS USA, a leading beef and pork processor in the US and Canada and the second-largest poultry company in the US and Mexico.[178]

Another reason for such public-private overlap is the massive political funding and lobbying efforts on behalf of carnistic industry. For example, in 2018 the livestock industry contributed over $6 million to congressional candidates. (And often, much of the contributions from agribusiness giants ends up going to those on the House and Senate agriculture committees.)[179] Lobbyists promote their clients' agenda to legislators. The success of lobbyists' efforts depends largely on the strength of their relationship with government officials; the more lobbyists can afford to provide politicians with niceties ranging from extravagant vacations to exclusive career opportunities, the stronger their relationship with those they seek to influence.

Put simply, carnistic industry can influence legislation to benefit itself, at great cost to us. Consider, for example, how the law requires that animal agribusinesses clean up at least some of the mess they've made after dumping their wastes—and yet it doesn't stipulate that these multibillion-dollar corporations cover the bill for their own cleanup. The Environmental Quality Incentives Program (EQIP), a federal program that was ostensibly created to help improve the environmental quality and practices of farmlands and farmers, subsidizes the cleanup. EQIP has doled out $113 million (11 percent of its funds) to help agricultural corporations neutralize the wastes they've dumped.[180] In other words, we help foot the bill for the damage done by corporations such as ConAgra, whose CEO earned $14.4 million in fiscal year 2019.[181] Animal agribusiness subsidies have been criticized by those across the political spectrum as one of the most egregious corporate welfare programs in the history of the United States.

Consider, too, the USDA's gross mismanagement of the deadly E. coli public health threat in 2002. Children who had eaten contaminated hamburgers became infected with the bacteria. Symptoms of E. coli infection include fever, vomiting, defecating blood, bruising, bleeding from the nose and mouth, swelling of the face and hands, high blood pressure, and, eventually, renal failure. Both ConAgra—the company that had sold the beef—and the USDA had allegedly known the meat was contaminated, yet took no action until two years later, when a full-blown outbreak forced the recall of nineteen million pounds of meat that had already been released into the nation's food supply.[182]

If your child were one of those who had become ill from eating contaminated beef, you might want to warn others about the safety of their meat. And this course of action might be effective—as long as you don't make the mistake Oprah Winfrey did and reach too many people at once. In 1996, Winfrey was sued for over $10 million by a group of Texas beef producers for libeling beef. At the height of the mad cow scare in Britain, when twenty people had died from eating what was believed to be tainted beef, Winfrey claimed, on the air, that she would not eat another burger. Under the "food libel laws," legislation that predated the Winfrey case and has been backed by agricultural corporations, it is illegal to criticize certain foods without producing "reasonable" scientific evidence. So you might find that, when it comes to speaking out about carnistic industry, some restrictions may apply—most notably those on your First Amendment rights.

When animal agribusinesses have become so powerful that they are not only above the law, but also of the law—shaping rather than respecting legislation—we can safely say our democracy has become a meatocracy.

SURGEON GENERAL'S WARNING: EATING CARNISTIC PRODUCTS MAY BE HAZARDOUS TO YOUR HEALTH

If you walked into your local convenience store and bought a package of cigars, you would notice that it carries a label warning of the potential dangers of cigar smoke. Yet research suggests that cigar smoking poses a hazard only to moderate to heavy cigar smokers, who comprise less than 1 percent[184] of the US population. More than 97 percent of adults,[185] however, eat carnistic products, and despite much research demonstrating the connection between the consumption of such products and disease, we are not warned of these dangers.

> According to a study published under the Disease Control Priorities Project, a joint enterprise of groups including the World Health Organization, the National Institutes of Health, and the World Bank, more than 90 percent of type 2 diabetes, 80 percent of coronary artery disease, 70 percent of strokes, and 70 percent of colon cancers may be prevented by a combination of lifestyle factors, including consuming a healthy, plant-based (vegan) diet.[183]

But let's imagine that you walked into that same convenience store to buy a hot dog. Now imagine that the US Department of Public Health had reviewed studies from the Harvard School of Public Health and other major research institutions and saw fit to include a warning label on carnistic products. The label might read something like this:

Surgeon General's Warning: Eating just one serving per day of unprocessed red meat can increase your risk of developing type 2 diabetes by 12 percent, eating one serving per day of processed red meat can increase it by 32 percent, and eating more than 28 grams of fish per day can increase it by 32 percent.[186] **Surgeon General's Warning:** Eating more than five eggs per week can increase your risk of developing colon cancer by 42 percent and eating more than two and a half eggs per week can increase your risk of developing prostate cancer by more than 81 percent.[187] **Surgeon General's Warning:** Eating poultry raises cholesterol levels similarly to red meat, increasing your risk of heart disease and stroke.[188] **Surgeon General's Warning:** If you've been diagnosed with prostate cancer, consuming more than three servings a day of dairy products can increase your chances of dying from the disease by 141 percent.[189] **Surgeon General's Warning:** The animal who became your meat may have been fed euthanized cats and dogs; rendered feathers, hooves, hair, skin, blood, and intestines; road kill; animal manure; plastic pellets that were harvested from dead cows' rumen; and carcasses from animals of their own species. **Surgeon General's Warning:** This product may contain dangerous levels of pesticides, arsenic, antibiotics, and hormones. **Surgeon General's Warning:** This product may contain microbial organisms that could lead to illness or death.[190] **Surgeon General's Warning:** Production of this food has contributed to serious environmental degradation, animal cruelty, and human rights violations. **Surgeon General's Warning:** There is shit in your meat.

But, of course, carnistic products come with no such warnings, despite the fact that these foods are consumed by hundreds of millions of people on a regular basis. Violent ideologies follow their own logic, the logic that sustains the system—a convoluted logic that unravels when it, itself, is labeled.

As we've discussed, the most notable characteristic of all violent ideologies is invisibility, both symbolic (by not being named) and literal (by keeping the violence out of sight). I have, therefore, attempted to illuminate the hidden aspects of carnism, so that you might understand the truth about the production of meat, eggs, and dairy and why the system works so diligently to remain unseen.

Yet invisibility can only protect us so much. Hints of the truth surround us: "cruelty-free" veggie burgers at the grocery store; the resilient vein in the drumstick that's suddenly reminiscent of a living chicken; snapshots of meat-packing plants that occasionally make the news; vegan guests at dinner parties; dead piglets hanging in the windows of Chinatown markets; the hog on a spit at the company barbecue; and an endless supply of dead animals virtually everywhere we turn, in the form of meat. So when invisibility inevitably falters, we need a backup, something to protect us from the truth and to help us quickly recover should we suddenly begin to catch on to the disturbing reality of carnism. We must replace the *reality* of eating animals with the *mythology* of eating animals.

CHAPTER 5

The Mythology of Eating Animals: Justifying Carnism

If we believe absurdities, we shall commit atrocities.
—VOLTAIRE

*Unthinking respect for authority is
the greatest enemy of truth.*
—ALBERT EINSTEIN

It is a sunny afternoon, and the petting zoo outside the local grocery store has drawn its usual crowd. Children and their parents are pressed up against the wooden fence, some leaning over it with arms outstretched. I take out one of the carrots I brought for this occasion and offer it to a piglet, hoping to lure her close enough for me to pet her. For some reason, I always feel an urge to physically connect with the animals. It seems almost instinctive, the desire to touch, to pet them.

And I am not alone. I watch as wide-eyed children shriek with delight when a piglet accepts one of their offerings and they get a chance to steal a fleeting stroke of his cheek or head. I see the adults laugh affectionately as the baby animal unselfconsciously gobbles down his food, unfazed by the eager little hands around him. I notice the attention the lone cow is getting, beckoned from all sides. When she chooses, for no apparent reason, my fistful of grass, I am warmed. I pet her velvety nose as others cluster around me to touch her head and neck.

Even the chickens elicit interest and amusement. Children squat down to toss breadcrumbs through the openings in the fence, smiling openmouthed as the birds peck at the ground and occasionally pause with heads cocked to observe the crowd. Not surprisingly, the onlookers comment on how adorable the fuzzy chicks are as they peep and hop around with no apparent focus.

It is a sight to behold. Children giggle and clap, mothers and fathers smile fondly, and everyone seems determined to touch and be touched by the pigs, cows, and chickens. Yet these people, who feel so deeply compelled to make contact with the animals, and who as children may have wept when they read *Charlotte's Web* and fallen asleep hugging their stuffed pigs or calves—these same people will soon leave the grocery store with bags containing beef, ham, chicken, and cheese. These people, who would undoubtedly rush to the aid of one of the barnyard animals were they suffering, are somehow not *outraged* that eleven billion of them are suffering needlessly every year, within the confines of an industry that is left entirely unaccountable for its actions.

Where has our empathy gone?

THE THREE NS OF JUSTIFICATION

In order to consume the meat, eggs, or dairy of the very species we had caressed but minutes before, we must believe so fully in the justness of eating animals that we are spared the consciousness of what we are doing. To this end, we are taught to accept a series of myths that maintain the carnistic system and to ignore the inconsistencies in the stories we tell ourselves. Violent ideologies rely on promoting fiction as fact and discouraging any critical thinking that threatens to expose this truth.

There is a vast mythology surrounding eating animals, but all the myths are in one way or another related to what

I refer to as the Three Ns of Justification: eating animals is *normal, natural,* and *necessary.* The Three Ns have been invoked to justify virtually all exploitative systems, from African slavery to the Nazi Holocaust. When an ideology is in its prime, these myths rarely come under scrutiny. However, when the system finally collapses, the Three Ns are recognized as ludicrous. Consider, for instance, the following justifications for why women were denied the right to vote in the United States: male-only voting was "designed by our forefathers"; if women were to vote, it would "cause irreparable damage . . . to the state" and "disaster and ruin would take over the nation."[191]

The Three Ns are so ingrained in our social consciousness that they guide our actions without our even having to think about them. They think for us. We have internalized them so fully that we often live in accordance with their tenets as though they were universal truths rather than widely held opinions. It's like driving a car—once you've learned to do it, you no longer need to think about every action. But these justifications do more than just direct our actions. They alleviate the moral discomfort we might otherwise feel when eating animals; if we have a good excuse for our behaviors, we feel less guilty about them. The Three Ns essentially act as mental and emotional blinders, masking the discrepancies in our beliefs and behaviors toward animals and explaining them away if we do happen to catch on.

MEET THE MYTHMAKERS

Despite the falsehoods that weave our psychological and emotional safety net, it takes energy to suppress the truth. It takes an ongoing effort to remain unaware of what is right in front of us, to stay oblivious to the glaring inconsistencies, and to keep our authentic feelings from surfacing. So, though we have become adept at ignoring the part of us that knows the truth, we must be continually coached to maintain the disconnection between our knowledge and our empathy.

Enter the mythmakers. The mythmakers occupy every sector of society, ensuring that no matter where we turn, the information we're given reinforces the Three Ns. The mythmakers are the institutions that form the pillars of the system, and the people who represent them. When a system is entrenched, it is supported by every major institution in society, from medicine to education; chances are, your doctors and teachers didn't encourage you to question whether eating animals is normal, natural, and necessary. Nor did your parents, pastor, or elected officials. Who better to influence us than the establishments and professionals in whom we have learned to place our trust? Who better to convince us than those in positions of authority?

Indeed, professionals play a key role in sustaining violent ideologies. One way they do this is by modeling the tenets of the ideology. In the case of carnism, professionals model attitudes and practices toward animals with their policies and recommendations—and their own behaviors. Consider, for instance, the neutral stance of the American Veterinary Medical Association (AVMA)—the "voice of the veterinary community"—regarding the use of gestation crates, two-foot-wide stalls in which sows are confined during pregnancy.[192] As I mentioned in chapter 3, these enclosures are considered so inhumane they've been banned in a number of nations and states, and even corporations such as McDonalds oppose them. Consider, too, that many veterinarians eat and wear animals.

Professionals also model the tenets of carnism by acting as "voices of reason," as "rational moderates"[193] in the debate about how animals should be treated. These people have been called "socialized critics"[194] because they lend credibility to the system by supporting the overall ideology while opposing some of its mores. The rational moderate stance of professionals makes those who challenge the system appear to be "irrational extremists" by contrast. A common example of rational moderates is veterinarians who oppose certain factory farming practices but regularly eat animals.

Another way professionals help sustain a violent ideology is by pathologizing or thwarting those who don't support it, as with psychologists who assume that a young woman's refusal to eat animals is symptomatic of an eating disorder or doctors who warn of the dangers of a vegan diet despite much evidence to the contrary. However, though professional support is essential for maintaining carnism, in general, professionals themselves don't consciously bolster the ideology. Professionals are simply people doing their jobs; they are people who were raised within the system and therefore, like the rest of us, see the world through the lens of carnism.

But not all mythmakers are unaware of the stories they spin. Another group of mythmakers, the animal agribusinesses and their executives, actively sustains the myths of carnism by influencing the institutions and professionals that in turn impact policy and opinion. Consider, for instance, the partnership between the Academy of Nutrition and Dietetics and the National Dairy Council.[195] The Academy is the nation's leading organization of nutritionists, and it is also the governing body that oversees the accreditation of universities that offer degrees in dietetics; all registered dietitians are required to have graduated from an Academy-accredited institution. (Thus, when we study nutrition, we actually study carnistic nutrition.)

The National Dairy Council is one of the Academy's leading "corporate sponsors." According to the Academy, their Corporate Sponsorship Program helps corporations have "access to key influencers, thought leaders and decision makers in the food and nutrition marketplace." And, the Academy says, the sponsor "can leverage benefits to achieve marketing objectives . . . gain access to food and nutrition leaders who influence and make critical purchasing decisions . . . [and] build brand relevance with [the Academy's] highly-desirable target audience."[196] In other words, institutional powerholders such as the National Dairy Council "sponsor" professional institutions like the Academy—which may help to explain, for instance, the official recommended daily allowance of three cups of milk, despite evidence linking dairy consumption with an increased risk of cardiovascular disease, various cancers, and diabetes.[197]

However, though the mythmakers distort the truth, their primary role lies not in creating myths, but in making sure the existing ones continue to thrive. So they function largely as *emissaries* of the myths. Many of the myths of carnism have been inherited, passed down through the generations; because systems are greater than the sum of their parts, they don't die a natural death, but live on indefinitely. Systems are like beehives: even though individual bees die, the swarm persists. The mythmakers thus recycle the myths of carnism, amending them when necessary to fit the current trend.

QUESTIONING AUTHORITY

Stanley Milgram's now-classic study on obedience to authority demonstrates just how vulnerable we are to authority figures. In the early 1960s, Milgram recruited forty male participants and told them that they would act as "teachers" in an experiment on the effects of punishment on learning. When each participant arrived, he was paired with another participant, a "learner." Unbeknown to the teachers, the learners were actually Milgram's accomplices. The pair was taken to a room where the learner was strapped to a chair and hooked up to what appeared to be electrodes. The men were told that the teacher was to call out word pairs for the learner to memorize, and if the learner didn't memorize them correctly, he'd be shocked by the teacher. With each subsequent mistake, the shock would increase in intensity. The teacher was taken to another room, which had an electric console that supposedly connected to the electrodes on the learner. On the console the shock voltages ranged from 15 to 450, and next to the highest voltage a sign read "Danger—Severe Shock."

In the beginning stages of the experiment, the learner remembered the word pairs accurately. But eventually, he started making mistakes. With the first few shocks, the learner groaned and made sounds of discomfort. By 150 volts, the learner was complaining that he was in pain and insisted on being released from the experiment. At 285 volts, the learner screamed in agony. All during this time, Milgram was instructing the teacher to continue. And most of the teachers did—a staggering thirty-four of the forty participants shocked the learner even after he had demanded to be released, and twenty-six of those thirty-four continued the shocks all the way up to 450 volts. The teachers were clearly in distress, sweating, holding their heads, complaining—and yet they continued. Milgram repeated his experiment again and again, with different groups and in different contexts, and each time the results were the same. He concluded that *obedience to authority overrides one's conscience.*

Milgram's conclusion is chilling, but not surprising. History is replete with examples of atrocities ranging from unjust wars to genocides, all of which were made possible by millions of people who followed the dictates of their leaders, people whose consciences had been deactivated by those in positions of authority.

Milgram did, however, find that there are two mitigating factors in one's obedience to authority: the ability to question the legitimacy of the authority figure and the distance one has from the figure. For instance, when Milgram had an "ordinary man" (one who seemed not to be a researcher) give the commands to administer shocks, obedience dropped by two-thirds; participants saw the researcher more as an equal than an authority. And when the researcher wasn't in the room with the teacher, obedience also dropped by two-thirds; the teachers would cheat.

Milgram believes that we act against our conscience because when a command comes from someone we perceive to be a legitimate authority, we don't see ourselves as fully responsible for our actions. And the closer in proximity this person is to us—whether it's a doctor giving us dietary advice or a celebrity on the television set in our living room telling us that "milk does a body good"—the more likely their authority will override our own. Until we learn to question external authority and acknowledge our own, internal authority, we will follow the decrees of those who maintain the status quo.*

* Different studies on obedience to authority, conducted by Milgram and by others, suggest that there is no appreciable difference between the responses of men and women.[198]

THE OFFICIAL SEAL OF
APPROVAL: LEGITIMATION

> The [Nazi] destruction process required the cooperation of
> every sector of German society. The bureaucrats drew up
> the definitions and decrees; the churches gave evidence of
> Aryan descent; the postal authorities carried the messages
> of deportation; business corporations dismissed their Jewish
> employees and took over . . . properties; the railroads carried
> the victims to their place of execution . . . the operation
> required and received the participation of every major social,
> political and religious institution of the German Reich.
>
> —RICHARD RUBENSTEIN, theologian

The practical goal of the myths is to *legitimize* the system. When an ideology is legitimized, its tenets are sanctioned by all social institutions and the Three Ns are disseminated through all social channels. Acting in accordance with the ideology is lawful, and it is considered reasonable and ethical. Consequently, the tenets of competing ideologies are viewed as *il*legitimate, which is why, for instance, vegans cannot press charges against agribusiness owners for the slaughtering of animals.

Though all institutions help legitimize the ideology, two in particular play a critical role: the legal system and the news media. Writing the tenets of an ideology into law forces conformity to the system. Consider, for instance, how the legal status of animals ensures continued carnistic production. Under US law, one can be either a legal *person* or legal *property*. A legal person is entitled to basic rights, most notably the right to live free from being physically violated by another. In contrast, legal property has no rights; only the legal person who owns the property has rights, which is why, for instance, you can sue someone who damages your car, but the car itself cannot press charges. Today, all humans are legal persons (though the Constitution originally classified slaves as three-fifths persons, two-fifths property), and all animals are legal property—and person-owners have the right to do what they will with their private property, with few exceptions. So animals are bought and sold, eaten and worn—and their bodies are used in such a wide variety of products that it's virtually impossible not to conform to the system. Animal by-products can be found in such unexpected commodities as tennis balls, wallpaper, adhesive bandages, and film.

The news media, our primary source of information, bolster carnism by acting as a direct channel from the ideology to the consumer. When it comes to carnism, the media often fail to challenge the system and support carnistic defenses: they maintain the invisibility of the system and reinforce the justifications for eating animals. (Fortunately, this trend is changing as more and more media professionals are acting as vegan allies—using their influence to challenge, rather than bolster, carnism.)

One way the media maintain carnistic invisibility is through *omission*. The eleven billion animals who are killed every year for human consumption and the virulent consequences of contemporary animal agricultural practices remain conspicuously absent from public discourse. How often have you seen media exposés on the violent treatment of farmed animals and the corrupt practices of carnistic industry? Compare this with the amount of coverage afforded fluctuating gas prices or Hollywood fashion blunders. Most of us are more outraged over having to pay five cents more for a gallon of gas than over the fact that billions of animals, millions of humans, and the entire ecosystem are systematically exploited by an industry that profits from such gratuitous violence. And most of us know more about what the stars wore to the Oscars than we do about the animals we eat.

The media also maintain the invisibility of the system through *prohibition,* through actively preventing information that challenges carnism from reaching consumers. For instance, in 2004, CBS turned down $2 million from the animal rights group People for the Ethical Treatment of Animals (PETA), which wanted to air an anticarnism advertisement during the Super Bowl. The network claimed the station didn't air "advocacy advertisements." However, CBS did run an antismoking advertisement during the game, and the station regularly airs commercials that promote carnistic consumption.

Sometimes, however, carnistic production does get media attention. But when this happens, the issue is usually presented as if it were an aberration rather than the norm. For example, in the exposé of a meatpacking plant in which sick animals had been processed and included in schoolchildren's meat that we discussed in chapter 3, there was no mention of the fact that the facility had been *randomly* targeted by Humane Society of the United States investigators, nor was there discussion of the potential prevalence of this practice among carnistic corporations. Thus, public outrage was directed toward only a single company, and the system itself remained unchallenged.

Indeed, the system remains unchallenged whenever the media present the tenets of carnism as fact rather than opinion, and the proponents of carnism as objective truthtellers rather than biased mythmakers. Major media venues, for instance, regularly feature segments on how to celebrate holidays that are organized around carnistic consumption, explaining how to prepare a traditional Thanksgiving turkey or host a Fourth of July cookout. And the doctors and nutritionists who appear in the media frequently advocate carnism, often assuming a "reasonable moderate" stance by, for example, recommending that viewers replace fatty meats with leaner meats.

The news media deliver carnism to our doorstep by informing us not only of "the way things are," but also of the way things ought to be, are meant to be, and have to be. In other words, the news media bring home the Three Ns.

EATING ANIMALS IS NORMAL

Custom will reconcile people to any atrocity.
—GEORGE BERNARD SHAW

When we view the tenets of an ideology as normal, it means the ideology has become *normalized,* and its tenets *social norms.* Social norms aren't merely descriptive—describing how the majority of people behave—they are also prescriptive, dictating how we *ought to* behave. Norms are socially constructed. They aren't innate, and they don't come from God (though some of us may have been taught otherwise); they are created and maintained by people, and they serve to keep us in line so the system remains intact.

Norms keep us in line by laying out paths for us to follow and by teaching us how to be so that we fit in. The path of the norm is the path of least resistance;[199] it is the route we take when we're on autopilot and don't even realize we're following a course of action that we haven't consciously chosen. Most people who eat animals have no idea that they're behaving in accordance with the tenets of a system that has defined many of their values, preferences, and behaviors. What they call "free choice" is, in fact, the result of a narrowly constructed set of options that have been chosen for them. They don't realize, for instance, that they have been taught to value human life so far above certain forms of nonhuman life that it seems appropriate for their taste preferences to supersede other species' preference for survival. And by carving out the path of least resistance, norms obscure alternative paths and make it seem as if there is no other way to be; as I mentioned in chapter 2, eating animals is considered a given, not a choice.

Another way norms keep us in line is by rewarding conformity and punishing us if we stray off course. Practically and socially, it is easier to eat animals than not. Carnistic products are readily available, while vegan alternatives must be actively sought out and may be hard to come by (though it's becoming increasingly easier to obtain vegan foods). For example, many restaurants still have no vegan options listed on the menu, and standard vegan fare, such as beans and rice, is frequently cooked with lard and chicken broth. And vegans often find themselves having to explain their choices, defend their diet, and apologize for inconveniencing others. They are stereotyped as radicals, eating disordered, and sometimes antihuman. They are called hypocrites if they wear leather, purists or extremists if they don't. They must live in a world where they are constantly bombarded by imagery and attitudes that offend their deepest sensibilities. It is easier by far to conform to the carnistic majority than eschew the path of least resistance.

Norms are reflected in everyday behavior, as well as in customs and traditions. When a behavior is customary or traditional, its longevity and role in maintaining the system make it less likely to be questioned and far easier to justify. For instance, for many people, Thanksgiving simply wouldn't be Thanksgiving without a turkey on the table; rarely is the choice of holiday fare questioned.

EATING ANIMALS IS NATURAL

Natural selection [has done much] for the progress of civilization. . . . The more civilised so-called Caucasian races have beaten the Turkish hollow in the struggle for existence. Looking to the world at no very distant date,

what an endless number of the lower races will have been
eliminated by the higher civilized races throughout the world.
—CHARLES DARWIN

Most of us believe that eating animals is natural because humans have consumed animals for millennia. And it is true that we have been eating animals as part of an omnivorous diet for at least two million years (though for the majority of this time our diet was still primarily vegan). But to be fair, we must acknowledge that infanticide, murder, rape, and cannibalism are at least as old as eating animals, and are therefore arguably as "natural"—and yet we don't invoke the longevity of these acts as a justification for them. As with other acts of violence, when it comes to eating animals, we must differentiate between natural and justifiable.

The way "natural" translates to "justifiable" is through the process of *naturalization*. Naturalization is to natural as normalization is to normal. When an ideology is naturalized, its tenets are believed to be in accordance with the laws of nature (and/or the law of God, depending on whether one's belief system is science- or faith-based, or both). Naturalization reflects a belief in the way things are *meant to* be; eating animals is seen as simply following the natural order of things. Naturalization maintains an ideology by providing it with a (bio)logical basis.

Like norms, many naturalized behaviors are constructed, and it should come as no surprise that they're constructed by those who place themselves at the top of the "natural hierarchy." The belief in the biological superiority of certain groups has been used for centuries to justify violence: Africans were "naturally" suited to slavery; Jews were "naturally" evil and would destroy Germany if not eradicated; women were "naturally" designed to be the property of men; animals "naturally" exist to be eaten by humans. Consider, for instance, how we refer to the animals we eat as though nature designed them for this very purpose: we call them "farm" (rather than "farm*ed*") animals, "broiler chickens," "dairy cows," "layer hens," and "veal calves." Even the great logician Aristotle invoked biology and bent logic to suit the norms of his era, when he asserted that males were naturally superior to females and slaves were biologically designed to serve free men. And consider one of the central justifications for carnism, the natural order of the so-called food chain. Humans supposedly reside at the "top" of the food chain—yet a chain, by definition, doesn't have a top; and if it did, it would be inhabited by carnivores, not omnivores.

The key disciplines that support naturalization are history, religion, and science. History presents us with a selective historical focus and "facts" that prove the ideology has always existed. The historical lens *eternalizes* the ideology, making it seem as if it always has been, and therefore always will be, the way things are. Religion upholds the ideology as divinely ordained, and science provides the ideology with a biological basis. The importance of religion and science in naturalizing an ideology helps to explain why spirituality and intelligence have been popular criteria by which a group defines itself as naturally superior. For instance, before animal experimentation was a common scientific practice, the mathematician and philosopher René Descartes nailed the paws of his wife's dog to a board in order to dissect him alive and prove that, unlike humans but like other animals, the dog was a soulless "machine" whose cries of pain were no different from the springs and wheels of a clock automatically reacting when dismantled. And Charles Darwin argued that because males were supposedly born with a greater capacity for reason than females, over the course of evolution men have become superior to women. In short, naturalization makes the ideology historically, divinely, and biologically irrefutable.

EATING ANIMALS IS NECESSARY

The belief that eating animals is necessary is closely connected to the belief that eating animals is natural; if eating animals is a biological imperative, then it is a necessity for the survival of the (human) species. And, as with all violent ideologies, this belief reflects the core paradox of the system: killing is necessary for the greater good; the survival of one group depends on the killing of another.[200] The belief that eating animals is necessary makes the system seem inevitable—if we cannot exist without eating animals, then abolishing carnism is akin to suicide. Though we know that it's possible to survive without eating animals, the system proceeds as if the myth of carnistic necessity were true; this myth reflects an implicit assumption that is typically only revealed when challenged.

A related myth is that eating animals is necessary for our health. This myth, too, persists in the face of overwhelming evidence to the contrary. If anything, research suggests that eating animals is *detrimental* to health, as carnistic consumption has been connected with the development of some of the major diseases of the industrialized world.

THE PROTEIN MYTH

But where do you get your protein?

This is often the first response a vegan hears after disclosing their dietary orientation. In fact, this question is so common as to be a running joke among vegans around the world. I use the term "joke" because the question reflects one of, if not the, most common and unrealistic myths about carnism: that meat (and to some degree eggs and dairy) is a necessary source of protein. Vegans refer to this misconception as the Protein Myth.

The fear of becoming protein deficient is especially common among men, as (animal) protein has traditionally been associated with building muscle and strength. Meat has long been a symbol of masculinity, as it represents power, might, and virility; conversely, plant-based foods have been feminized, often representing passivity and weakness (consider the meaning of the phrases "couch potato" and "veg out"). There is a growing body of literature examining how masculinity has been constructed— to the detriment of individuals and society—largely around dominance, control, and violence. It should come as no surprise, then, that consuming (and sometimes killing) animals has been a central feature of manhood.[201]

Like other myths of carnism, the Protein Myth exists in the face of longstanding, widespread, and substantial evidence to the contrary; it acts to justify continued carnistic consumption and maintain the carnistic paradigm. But it is, indeed, a myth. Here's what doctors have to say:

> In the early 1900s, Americans were told to eat well over 100 grams of protein a day. And as recently as the 1950s, health-conscious people were encouraged to boost their protein intake. Today . . . Americans tend to take in twice the amount of protein they need. Excess protein has been linked with osteoporosis, kidney disease, calcium stones in the urinary tract, and some cancers.
>
> People build muscle and other body proteins from amino acids, which come from the proteins they eat. A varied diet of beans, lentils, grains, and vegetables contains all of the essential amino acids. It was once thought that various plant foods had to be eaten together to get their full protein value, but current research suggests this is not the case.
>
> To consume a diet that contains enough, but not too much, protein, [one can] simply replace carnistic products with grains, vegetables, legumes (peas, beans, and lentils), and fruits. As long as one is eating a variety of plant foods in sufficient quantity to maintain one's weight, the body gets plenty of protein.[202]

One particularly striking myth of necessity is the belief that we must continue to eat animals because if we were to stop now, the world would be overrun by pigs, chickens, and cows. What, we wonder, would we do with all the animals? Of course, if we stopped eating carnistic products, we'd stop producing the animals who become such products in the first place, so we'd be safe from being overwhelmed by a burgeoning population of farmed animals. And there is a myth within this myth, a paradox that is central to all violent ideologies—that killing must continue in order to justify all the killing already done.[203] Once the momentum of the violence has reached a certain point, reversing it seems impossible.

Another myth of necessity is that killing is an economic imperative. While an economic motive *has* driven many violent ideologies—the economy of the New World was largely buttressed by slavery, and the plundering of gold and other assets as well as the unpaid labor of Nazi victims financed the German war machine—that doesn't mean the economy would collapse were the killing to cease. It is far more likely that the *economic status quo* would break down; the carnistic-corporate power structure, rather than the populace, would suffer were carnism abolished.

Even were the economy dependent on carnism, one must wonder whether this dependence would justify the continued violence. For most people, it would not. History shows us again and again that, when people become aware of violent ideologies, they demand change. It is for this reason that the atrocities of carnism must remain hidden and the myths of carnism must remain intact—that we must believe we are informed consumers and free agents acting within a democratic system, exercising our own free will.

THE MYTH OF FREE WILL

Violent ideologies require willing participants, and most people would not willingly harm animals. Thus, we must be coerced into supporting the system. However, coercion is effective only as long as it remains undetected. We must believe we are acting entirely of our own volition when we purchase and consume the bodies of animals; we must believe in the Myth of Free Will.

Of course, nobody's putting a gun to our heads when we eat animals, but they don't have to. From the moment we were weaned, we were eating animals. Did you freely choose to eat your Gerber Turkey and Rice Dinner? How about when you were a child, eating your McDonald's Happy Meal? And did you question your parents and teachers and doctors when they told you milk made you strong? Did you ever look at the meatballs atop your pasta and wonder where they really came from? If so, did the people around you encourage you to close the gap in your consciousness, or did they quickly restore your numbing and reassure you of the virtues of eating animals?

Chances are, the pattern by which you have related to carnistic products started before you were old enough to talk and has continued uninterrupted throughout your life. And it is in this flow of uninterrupted behavior that we may see how carnism washes over free will. Patterns of thought and action, established long before we were able to operate as free agents, become woven into the fabric of our psyche, guiding our choices like an invisible hand. And if something should interrupt our habitual way of relating to carnistic products— if, for instance, we catch a glimpse of the slaughter process— the elaborate network that makes up the defensive structure of carnism pulls us swiftly back in. *Carnism blocks interruptions in consciousness.*

It is impossible to exercise free will as long as we are operating from within the system. Free will requires consciousness, and our pervasive and deep-seated patterns of thought are unconscious; they are outside of our awareness and therefore outside of our control. While we remain in the system, we see the world through the eyes of carnism. And as long as we look through eyes other than our own, we will be living in accordance with a truth that is not of our own choosing. We must step outside the system to find our lost empathy and make choices that reflect what we truly feel and believe, rather than what we've been taught to feel and believe.

CHAPTER 6

Through the Carnistic Looking Glass: Internalized Carnism

The greatest enemy of knowledge is not ignorance; it is the illusion of knowledge.
—STEPHEN HAWKING

Imagine if everything that constitutes your reality—your home, your job, your family, your *life*—were nothing more than an illusion, a virtual reality, fabricated by a computerized matrix that your brain and the brains of all other humans were plugged into. Imagine this matrix uses us as batteries; it siphons off our energy to keep itself alive and keeps us complacent by remaining invisible while generating the illusion of our freedom. Such is the theme of *The Matrix*, a film that resonated so powerfully with millions of viewers that it was heralded as a modern classic. Classics attain their status because they speak to a core human experience. They give voice to truths that have been largely elusive and thus unspoken. *The Matrix* challenges us to question—to question what we see, and how we relate to what we see. It challenges us to be curious about what we think and why we think the way we do. Morpheus, a leading character in the film, explains to the protagonist, Neo:

> The Matrix is everywhere. It is all around us. Even now, in this very room. You can see it when you look out your window or when you turn on your television. You can feel it when you go to work . . . when

you go to church . . . when you pay your taxes. It is the world that has been pulled over your eyes to blind you to the truth . . . [it is] a prison for your mind.

Neo's mind was imprisoned by a matrix, a system so entrenched that it had effectively stripped him of the ability to think for himself. And by accepting the illusions of the Matrix as real, Neo helped authenticate the system; he was at once prisoner and captor, victim and perpetrator.

Likewise, the matrix that is carnism compels us to participate in our own coercion, doing the system's job for it: we deny, avoid, and justify carnism. When our minds are imprisoned by carnism, we see the world—and ourselves—through the eyes of the system. As a result, we behave not as we actually are, but as the system would like us to be: we are passive consumers rather than active citizens. The mechanisms of the system have become ingrained into our consciousness. We have *internalized* carnism.

THE COGNITIVE TRIO

Carnism distorts reality: Just because we don't see the animals we eat, this doesn't mean they don't exist. Just because the system hasn't been named, this doesn't mean it isn't real. No matter how far they stretch and how deep they run, the myths of eating animals are not the facts of eating animals.

Internalized carnism distorts our *perception* of reality: though animals are living beings, we perceive them as living things; though they are individuals, we perceive them as abstractions— as a "bunch" of things; and in the absence of any objective, supporting data, we perceive them as though their appropriateness for human consumption is naturally contingent upon their species. For instance, if, despite the system's best efforts, we happen to catch sight of one of the pigs who is to become our meat, we don't perceive him or her as a sentient being, or as someone who has a distinct personality and preferences. Rather, we perceive the pig's "pigness" (dirtiness, slovenliness, etc.) and his or her "edibility." By perceiving animals in these ways, we employ three defenses that I refer to as the Cognitive Trio.

The Cognitive Trio is comprised of *objectification, deindividualization,* and *dichotomization.* These defenses are actually normal psychological processes that become defensive distortions when used excessively, as they must be in order to keep carnism intact. And, unlike some other defenses, these mechanisms are more internal and less conscious and intentional; they are less about *what* we think than they are about *how* we think. Each defense in the Cognitive Trio has a unique effect on our perception of animals. But the true strength of the trio lies in how the three work in harmony with one another. Like a musical trio, the whole is greater than the sum of its parts.

OBJECTIFICATION: VIEWING ANIMALS AS THINGS

The more you see these lambs without any heads on them, the more you don't think of them as an animal, but as a product that you're working with.
—Thirty-one-year-old meat cutter*

Objectification is the process of viewing a living being as an inanimate object, a thing. Animals are objectified in a variety of ways, perhaps most notably through language. Objectifying language is a powerful distancing mechanism. Consider how slaughterhouse workers refer to the animals they're going to kill as the objects they are to become, rather than as the living animals they are: chickens are called *broilers,*

---

* Selected quotes in this chapter are from interviews I conducted for my doctoral dissertation on the psychology of eating meat.

pigs are called *rashers*, and bulls are called *beef*. And the USDA refers to cows as *udders* and animals as *units*, while carnistic producers talk about *replacement boars* or *replacement calves*. Consider, too, our common usage of the phrase *living thing*, and our equally common failure to recognize this phrase as an oxymoron. Carnism needs us to employ such objectifying language; think of how you might feel if, for instance, you referred to the rotisserie chicken in the restaurant window as some*one* rather than some*thing*, or if you called the octopus swimming behind the sushi bar *he or she* rather than *it*.

Objectification is legitimized not only through language, but also through institutions, legislation, and policies. For example, as we discussed in chapter 5, the law classifies animals as property. When we can buy, sell, trade, or exchange someone as though they were a used car—or even parts of a used car—we have literally turned them into a piece of live*stock*. By viewing animals as objects, we can treat their bodies accordingly, without the moral discomfort we might otherwise feel.

DEINDIVIDUALIZATION: VIEWING ANIMALS AS ABSTRACTIONS

I don't [think of farmed animals as individuals]. I wouldn't be able to do my job if I got that personal with them. . . . When you say individuals, you mean as a unique person, as a unique thing with its own name and its own characteristics, its own little games it plays? Yeah? Yeah, I'd really rather not know that. I'm sure it has it, but I'd rather not know it.
—Thirty-one-year-old meat cutter

Deindividualization is the process of viewing individuals only in terms of their group identity and as having the same characteristics as everyone else in the group. Whenever we encounter a group of others, it's natural for us to think of them, at least in part, as a group. The larger the group, the more likely we are to view the whole over its individual parts; when you think of a nation, for example, you probably think of its residents primarily as members of a group to which you've ascribed a set of shared characteristics. Deindividualization, however, is viewing others *only* as members of a whole; it is the failure to appreciate the individuality of the parts that make up the whole. Such is the case with our perception of the animals we eat.

For instance, as I mentioned previously, when you think of the pigs raised for pork you probably don't think of them as individuals with their own personalities and preferences. Rather, you see them as an *abstraction*, as a group. Like other groups that have been victims of violent ideologies, pigs raised for meat may have numbers rather than names and are considered no different from one another; a pig is a pig and all pigs are the same. But imagine how you would feel if your package of hot dogs included a label with the name, picture, and description of the pig from whom the meat was procured, or if you became acquainted with one of the pigs who was to become your food. Countless students of mine, as well as the meat eaters and meat cutters I interviewed for my research, reported that after getting to know an individual farmed animal, they felt unable to consume that particular animal, and some even felt uncomfortable continuing to eat meat from that species. For instance, a thirty-year-old meat cutter told me, "I would have a different outlook on pigs in general if I had a pig as a pet. I would just see my pet every time someone was preparing ribs or something like that."

Negative reactions to the idea of consuming (or preparing the meat of) a familiar animal are common around the world, and they can be quite powerful. For instance, female Indians from the Quito area in Ecuador bond with chickens just as Americans do with dogs and cats, and when circumstances force these women to sell their birds for slaughter, they do so with tears and shrieks.[204] And consider the responses of interviewees when I asked them how they would react to eating a farmed animal they'd become acquainted with. A thirty-five-year-old meat eater explained, "It would feel wrong to eat that [meat]. I mean, it would feel like I murdered it, you know, that I killed it. And for what? You know what I'm saying? I wouldn't even conceive of it. If it's a pet, it's off limits, you know? Once it dies, you bury it; it's sort of like a family member."

This feeling is echoed by a fifty-eight-year-old butcher, who told me, "I'd have to be starving before I'd eat my own pet [pig] [because] once I knew him or her really well I would be offended to have to eat my friend." Yet when I asked why he doesn't feel the same way about the pigs he processes for his job, he responded, "I must class them all as food. If someone was raising him as a pet, that would be different."

One meat eater, a thirty-one-year-old who had raised and killed his own animals in his native country, Zimbabwe, explained, "I would not eat something that I would give a name to. . . . For me, that's like your friend. You are eating an animal that you have a close relationship with."

Another meat eater, a twenty-eight-year-old, said that he would not even have to be personally acquainted with an animal to feel uncomfortable by their individuality: "Even, like, some animal in a cage with hundreds of other animals, if you make this connection [that they are an individual], then it's kind of on the same parallel as the family pet. How can you kill a family pet? How can you kill a pig that's in a pen with a hundred others?"

Recognizing the individuality of others interrupts the process of deindividualization, making it more difficult to maintain the psychological and emotional distance necessary to harm them.

NUMBERS AND NUMBING

Psychologist Paul Slovic examined the relationship between the number of victims in a traumatic situation and witnesses' responses to their suffering.[205] What he found was that the greater the number of victims, the more witnesses blurred, or deindividualized, them and the less the witnesses tended to care—and this blurring seemed to start at just two victims. Slovic argues that numbers and numbing go hand in hand. What this means is that individual victims, human or nonhuman, are much more likely to arouse our compassion than are groups of victims.

Consider, for instance, the 2005 incident in which a sparrow flew into a domino competition in the Netherlands, knocking over 23,000 tiles and ending up shot dead: a website was set up as a tribute to the bird, and it attracted tens of thousands of visitors. Or take the 2001 slaughtering of millions of bovines in the United Kingdom that were believed to have been exposed to hoof-and-mouth disease: despite the demands of animal activists to halt the killing, it wasn't until a newspaper printed a photo of a young calf named Phoenix that the government agreed to change its policy. And when author Annie Dillard told her seven-year-old daughter how it was hard for her to imagine that 138,000 people had drowned in Bangladesh, her daughter replied, "No, it's easy. Lots and lots of dots in blue water."

Mother Teresa was all too familiar with the phenomenon of numbers and numbing. "If I look at the mass," she said, "I will never act."

DICHOTOMIZATION: VIEWING ANIMALS IN CATEGORIES

I don't know; maybe it's easier to [eat] animals that have been raised just for the purpose of [being eaten] . . . where a squirrel runs around your backyard and then to have it on your dinner plate is just kind of disturbing. . . . It's almost like a division between the animals you see running around outside—they are safe from people eating [them].

—Twenty-two-year-old meat eater

Dichotomization is the process of mentally putting others into two, often opposing, categories based on our beliefs about them. In and of itself, classifying others into groups is not problematic. As we discussed in chapter 1, creating mental classifications is a natural process that helps us organize information. Dichotomies, however, are not just classifications; they are dualistic, and as such, they create a black-and-white picture of reality. What results is a divvying up of the world into inflexible, value-laden categories that are usually based on little or inaccurate information. Dichotomization thus enables us to separate groups of individuals in our minds and to harbor very different emotions toward them.

When it comes to carnism, the two main categories we have for animals are edible and inedible. And within the edible-inedible dichotomy, we have a number of other category pairs. For example, we eat domesticated rather than wild animals, and herbivores rather than omnivores or carnivores. Most people won't eat animals they deem intelligent (dolphins), but regularly consume those they believe are not very smart (tuna). Many people avoid eating animals they perceive as cute (rabbits) and instead eat animals they consider less attractive (turkeys).

Whether the categories into which we've placed animals are accurate is less important than whether we *believe* they're accurate, since the purpose of dichotomization is simply to distance us from the discomfort of eating animals. If we filter our perceptions of animals through categories laden with value judgments, we can, for example, eat our steak while we pet our dog and remain oblivious to the implications of our choices. Dichotomization thus supports justification; it enables us to feel justified eating an animal because, for instance, he or she isn't smart, isn't a pet, isn't cute—isn't edible.

Of course, not all edible animals fall neatly into the categories into which we've placed them. To maintain the carnistic status quo, then, we retain false assumptions about the animals we eat so that we can continue to classify them as edible. Intelligent pigs and chickens are seen as stupid, and handsome turkeys are viewed as ugly.

When pressed to examine our assumptions, however, the arbitrary and irrational nature of dichotomization becomes apparent. Consider, for instance, the confusion expressed by a forty-three-year-old meat eater when I asked him to explain why he doesn't eat lamb:

> [Lambs] are gentle creatures. . . . It's, like, a shame they are killed and we eat them. There are a lot of other things that are also gentle, too, that we eat . . . cows are. We eat them. . . . I don't know how to describe it. It seems like everybody eats cow. It's cheaper. It's affordable, and there are so many of them. But lambs are just different. They're smaller or more cuddly. I don't know. You don't cuddle a cow. Seems like it's okay to eat a cow, but it's not okay to eat a lamb. . . . The difference is weird.

TECHNOLOGY, DISTORTIONS, AND DISTANCING

It's easier to think of [farmed animals] in the abstract. . . .
It makes me think of that quote: "The death of one person
is a tragedy; the death of a group is a statistic."
—Thirty-three-year-old meat eater

A discussion about the Cognitive Trio would not be complete without mentioning the role of technology in psychological distortions and distancing. Technology reinforces the Trio by enabling us to treat certain animals as objects and abstractions—objects, because they literally become units of production on a disassembly line, and abstractions, because the sheer volume of animals killed under carnism inevitably deindividualizes them. Indeed, it is only because of technology that widescale carnistic production is possible: modern methods enable us to consume billions of animals every year without witnessing a single part of the process by which these animals become our food. This mass production of meat, eggs, and dairy, coupled with our removal from the production process, has made us at once more and less violent toward animals than ever before; we are able to kill more animals but are less desensitized to or comfortable with the fact that we're killing them. Technology has widened the gap between our behaviors and values, and thus enhanced the moral dissonance that the system works so hard to obscure.

But of course, technology often doesn't eradicate all traces of carnistic production. And when it doesn't, we can find ourselves in the uncomfortable position of recognizing that our food did, in fact, come from a living being. For instance, a twenty-two-year-old meat eater told me that she didn't eat pork from a market in her town that sold pigs' feet and whole pigs: "I think partially because it reminds me more that you're not just eating—like the piece of meat didn't just fall out of the sky. It's connected to the whole animal . . . instead of just a nicely processed thing that you're eating by itself for dinner. . . . You have to think about it as a whole creature."

DISTORTIONS AND DISGUST

I don't like to eat chicken hearts. . . . I think that it is mainly because [with] the chicken hearts, you can really see that it is a small heart. [If I ate it I'd feel] sick. . . . It's just what we associate the heart to be, and you know, the liver and things like that . . . someone's heart or liver—they're associated with people.
—Twenty-seven-year-old meat eater

By distorting our perceptions of animals, the Cognitive Trio prevents us from *identifying* with them. To identify with others is to see something of yourself in them and to see something of them in yourself—even if the only thing you identify with is the desire to be free from suffering. Identification is a cognitive process, and when we think of animals as objects, abstractions, or items in fixed categories, we diminish this process. And because thoughts affect feelings, the less we identify with others, the less we empathize with them. This is what's known in psychology as the similarity principle: we feel more empathy toward those whom we perceive to be more like us. Consider, for example, how you might be more disturbed by the deaths of people in a plane crash who came from your city than by the deaths of other passengers, even if you weren't personally acquainted with anyone on board. Consider, too, the statement of a fifty-eight-year-old butcher I interviewed:

I took my son in [to the butcher shop]—he is eight years old. We had a lamb in there. He likes lamb so he walks in and says, "What's that?"

I go, "That's a lamb."

No big deal, but a couple days later I asked, "Do you want a nice lamb steak?"

"Naw," he said, "I don't think I want lamb. I looked at that animal . . . [and] it was looking back at me."

Just as the degree to which we identify with another determines how much we empathize with them, the degree of our empathy determines, in large part, how disgusted we feel at the notion of eating them.* (Some possible exceptions are animals we mentally classify as disgusting even when they're alive, such as snakes and insects, and certain species we consider "dirty," like rats and pigeons.) The fact that identification and empathy inform disgust may explain why researchers have found that almost all disgusting objects are of animal origin (and those that are not of animal origin often resemble animal products, such as slimy, mucus-like okra). The following diagram represents the correlation between identification, empathy, and disgust:

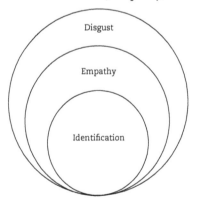

---

* While disgust is sometimes an innate response intended to protect us from ingesting harmful substances, such as feces and rotten vegetation, it can also be a reaction to purely ideational, or psychological, stimuli. Ideational disgust is the focus of this book.

The reason empathy and disgust are so closely connected is because empathy informs, to a large degree, our sense of morality, and disgust is a *moral emotion*. Typically, the more empathy we feel for an animal, the more immoral—and thus disgusted—we feel eating them. The connection between morality and disgust is supported by a number of studies that have shown that people feel disgusted by the idea of consuming a product that they find morally offensive, that violates their sense of integrity.[206] Consider the comment of a thirty-four-year-old meat eater who regularly enjoys eating meat, but is ethically opposed to eating veal: "Let's just say I came to your house . . . and you told me that I just had veal. I'd probably vomit . . . like I *have to* get that out of my system."

DISGUSTED BY INJUSTICE

An interesting study conducted by researchers at the University of Toronto suggests that we may be hardwired to feel disgusted by moral offenses.[207] The researchers attached electrodes to the faces of twenty participants, to record changes in their facial movements. The participants were then subjected to a series of three different conditions: they were given "disgusting" tasting liquids to drink; they looked at photos of disgusting things, such as dirty toilets and injuries; and they were subjected to unfair treatment in a laboratory game they played. The researchers found that in each condition, the subjects' automatic facial movements were the same: they contracted their levator labii muscle, which raises the upper lip and wrinkles the nose, indicating a disgust response. The researchers concluded that "moral disgust" may, in fact, be closely linked to the primal, ancient disgust response that protected us from eating rotting or contaminated foods. Other studies have yielded similar results.

PSYCHOLOGICAL DAMAGE CONTROL: DISGUST AND RATIONALIZATION

For any number of reasons, we may find ourselves disgusted by the meat, eggs, or dairy of edible animals—products that aren't supposed to disgust us. In such instances, when disgust breaks through the defenses that keep us numbed, we need a backup defense to act as a safety net; we need to rationalize the irrational.

Rationalization is the defense mechanism by which we provide a rational explanation for something that is not rational. As with other defenses, rationalization serves to keep the system intact. When the carnistic distancing process has been disrupted and disgust arises, we may divert attention from our moral discomfort by blaming our disgust on something other than the fact that we are consuming a living being. For example, when we feel disgusted by meat that reminds us of its animal source, we may attribute our aversion to the texture of the meat or to an imagined health risk. As one interviewee told me, "I don't like eating bacon because . . . it kind of grosses me out. . . . It's saturated with grease. I just can't imagine that being very good for my body. . . . To see that much grease and fat, even if it tasted good, I think it would repulse me." I asked her whether she felt the same way toward french fries, or other greasy foods, and she replied, "It's similar, but there's also something about seeing raw meat when you are cooking. . . . [C]ooking a potato isn't quite as bad, I think. . . . It's that certain connection that [the meat] is a piece of something, not just something that you got out of the ground."

And another interviewee explained, "I won't eat something that is raw or half raw. . . . The sight of blood—I don't like blood, so I sure don't want it running out of my food when I'm eating it." When I asked how the sight of bloody meat made him feel, he responded, "[It's] disgusting. It's not healthy, although I know it's probably more healthy to eat [it] rare than well done."

It is striking how an entire society of rational people can maintain such irrational patterns of thought without catching on to the gaping holes in the logic. And yet this paradox makes sense when understood within the context of carnism: because its modus operandi is to distort rather than report reality, the system is inherently irrational. And because we are looking at the system from within—from within a schema that mirrors it—we have adopted its logic as our own.

EMOTIONAL EATING

It is often believed that a culture's avoidance of consuming certain kinds of animals is rational, stemming from the culture's attempt to preserve itself. We assume, for instance, that a culture doesn't advocate eating animals that are unhealthy (think sewer-dwelling rats), useful (like oxen that plow fields), or uneconomical to raise and slaughter (such as carnivorous animals that would be dangerous to handle). However, while in some instances there may be a logical reason for a cultural taboo against consuming a particular type of animal, research suggests that more often, the opposite is true: cultures use explanations such as those above as a way to rationalize their irrational choices of which animals to eat.

In myriad cultures, many species of "edible" animals are perceived as inedible, which strongly suggests that cultural prejudice, rather than logic, determines which animals become classified as food. For example, the Nambikwara Indians of Brazil keep domesticated animals that would be suitable for human consumption, yet treat them instead as pets, interacting with them much as Americans do with dogs and cats; they don't even eat the eggs laid by their hens.[208] Furthermore, there's no reason why Americans shouldn't eat horses, as some French people do; or cockroaches, as some Asians do; or pigeons, which are plentiful and consumed in Egypt. Californians could easily harvest the snails that overpopulate their gardens and are the same species as those served as escargots, but they choose instead to eat only imported snails.[209] And Asian horse people, who have been highly dependent on equines, have no prohibitions against consuming horseflesh. When it comes to deciding which species of animals to eat, it seems that emotion trumps reason.

PICKING OUT THE DOG MEAT: DISGUST AND CONTAMINATION

Disgust has what psychologists call contamination properties. In other words, something disgusting can render anything it comes in contact with disgusting as well. For instance, most of us will not eat soup that a fly has landed in, even if we were able to quickly remove the insect and the surrounding liquid it touched. The remaining soup, with no residual trace of the fly, has become irreparably contaminated. The soup itself wasn't disgusting, but the *idea* that something disgusting— a fly—touched even a small part of it has rendered the soup inedible.

You were first asked to consider the contaminating property of disgust in chapter 1, when you were presented with a scenario in which you were told you had been served dog meat and then were asked whether you would pick the meat out of the stew and just eat the vegetables around it. Chances are, if you had been disgusted by the dog meat, you would also have become disgusted by anything it touched. That is because, unlike *distaste*—disliking the flavor of a product— disgust is often *ideational*: it can be triggered by an idea or belief about a food rather than what that food actually is. The contaminating effect of disgust explains why many vegans feel unable to eat food that has been cooked with, or near, meat, eggs, or dairy.*

THE MATRIX WITHIN THE MATRIX: THE CARNISTIC SCHEMA

Carnism is a social system, a social matrix. But it is also a psychological system, a system of thought, an *internal* matrix. It is a matrix within the Matrix. And just as the social matrix is set up to maintain the gap in our consciousness, so, too, is the psychological matrix. This psychological matrix is what I call the *carnistic schema*. The carnistic schema is largely comprised of the Cognitive Trio, but it also includes the other defenses and beliefs discussed throughout this book. The carnistic schema is, essentially, the plug that connects us to the broader matrix of carnism.

You may recall from chapter 1 that a schema is the lens through which we view the world, and it serves as a mental classification system that organizes and interprets incoming information. The carnistic schema dictates which animals are edible

---

* An interesting phenomenon I have observed is that many vegans tend to be less disgusted by eggs and dairy products than they are by meat. Research on this phenomenon is lacking. However, I suspect that, because it seems like it should be possible to obtain eggs and dairy products without violence (even though doing so is, in fact, all but impossible), these foods are perceived as less morally offensive and thus less disgusting.

and which are inedible, and it determines how—or, more accurately, whether—we feel when we eat carnistic products.

Schemas, however, don't only *classify* information, they also *filter* information; we tend to notice and remember only that which confirms our preexisting assumptions. Psychologists refer to this phenomenon as *confirmation bias.* The carnistic schema selectively allows in information that maintains the gap in our consciousness, and it distorts our perception of information that threatens to close this gap. In other words, the carnistic schema determines what we notice, how we interpret what we notice, and whether we remember what we notice. For instance, during the classroom exercise that I described in chapter 2, in which my students shared their belief that pigs are stupid and disgusting, some of the students later admitted that they had at some point in their lives encountered information discrediting this belief. Yet such information had been quickly forgotten, as their carnistic schema pulled their original view of pigs back into place. Another example of confirmation bias is how the distress people feel upon witnessing footage of animals being slaughtered often "wears off" shortly thereafter.

TOLSTOY SYNDROME

The phenomenon psychologists refer to as "confirmation bias" has also been called Tolstoy syndrome, after the Russian author who wrote of our tendency to be blinded by our beliefs. As Tolstoy said:

> I know that most men, including those at ease with problems of the greatest complexity, can seldom accept the simplest and most obvious truth if it . . . would oblige them to admit the falsity of conclusions which they have . . . woven, thread by thread, into the fabrics of their life.

The carnistic schema, which twists information so that nonsense seems to make perfect sense, also explains why we fail to see the absurdities of the system. Consider, for instance, advertising campaigns in which pigs dance joyfully over the fire pit where they are to be barbecued, or chickens wear aprons while beseeching the viewer to eat them. And consider the Veterinarian's Oath of the American Veterinary Medical Association, "I solemnly swear to use my . . . skills for the . . . relief of animal suffering," in light of the fact that the vast majority of veterinarians eat animals simply because they like the way they taste. Or think about how people may refuse to replace their hamburgers with veggie burgers, even if the flavor is identical, because they claim that, if they try hard enough, they can detect a subtle difference in texture. Only when we deconstruct the carnistic schema can we see the absurdity of placing our preference for a flawless re-creation of a textural norm over the lives and deaths of billions of others.

THIS WAY OUT: THE CRACK IN THE CARNISTIC MATRIX

The carnistic system is riddled with absurdities, inconsistencies, and paradox. It is fortified by a complex network of defenses that make it possible for us to believe without questioning, to know without thinking, and to act without feeling. It is a coercive system that has cultivated in us an elaborate routine of mental gymnastics that keeps us from being grounded in our truth. Thus, one cannot help but wonder: *Why all the acrobatics?* Why must the system go to such lengths to keep itself intact?

The answer is simple. Because we care about animals, and we care about the truth. And because the system depends on our not caring, and the system is built on deception. Carnism is a house of cards, a fractured and fragmented system that needs a strong fortress to protect itself from its very own proponents—us.

And like the cinematic Matrix, the matrix of carnism can only imprison our minds and hearts as long as we guard our own cells, as long as we are willing participants. It can only block the truth as long as we can tolerate living a lie. As Morpheus explained to Neo:

> I see it in your eyes. You have the look of a man who accepts what he sees because he is expecting to wake up. . . . Let me tell you why you're here. You're here because you know something. What you know you can't explain, but you feel it. You've felt it your entire life, that there's something wrong with the world. You don't know what it is, but it's there, like a splinter in your mind. . . . I'm trying to free your mind, Neo. But I can only show you the door. You're the one who has to walk through it.

Like Neo, you're here, reading this book, because you've known something is wrong with the world. You are ready to step outside of the carnistic matrix and reclaim the empathy the system has worked so hard to protect you from, the very empathy that leads to the door of carnism—the empathy that will help you walk *through* that door to create a more just and compassionate world.

CHAPTER 7

Bearing Witness:
From Carnism to Compassion

In a dark time, the eye begins to see.
—THEODORE ROETHKE

Our grandchildren will ask us one day: Where
were you during the Holocaust of the animals?
What did you do against these horrifying crimes?
We won't be able to offer the same excuse
for the second time, that we didn't know.
—HELMUT KAPLAN

In November 1995, Emily the cow stood in a lineup of bovines in a New England slaughterhouse, awaiting her turn to pass through the swinging doors to the kill floor. Perhaps it was the smell of blood, or the fact that those who had gone before her didn't return, but Emily suddenly charged out of the line, sprinted toward the five-foot-high fence that corralled the grounds, and hefted her 1,500-pound body over the top. She fled through the woods and eluded the incredulous workers who chased after her.

For forty frigid days and nights, Emily hid from her pursuers in the wooded areas of Hopkinton, Massachusetts, a small rural town in the heart of New England. And though A. Arena & Sons, the owners of the slaughterhouse from which Emily escaped, were determined to capture her, the locals were determined to aid her in her flight to freedom. Farmers left out bales of hay for her; residents deliberately misled police by giving false information about her location.

Lewis and Megan Randa, founders of the nearby Peace Abbey, a spiritual and educational center for nonviolent living, learned of Emily's plight. The Randas offered to buy Emily from A. Arena & Sons. They hoped that Emily could live out her life in the small animal sanctuary on their grounds. The owner of the slaughterhouse, Frank Arena, was moved by Emily's story and agreed to sell the $500 cow for just $1. This unexpected act of benevolence was followed by another: film producer Ellen Little, who bought the rights to Emily's story for a sum that covered the cow's care for the rest of her life, donated an extra $10,000 to build a new barn for Emily and an adjacent educational center that focused on animal issues.

Emily, once an anonymous dairy cow, came to be an individual who inspired compassion in the many lives she touched. People from around the world reported that they stopped eating animals simply from learning about her. Their carnistic defenses broke down and were replaced by compassion. Why else would a community of meat eaters and farmers aid a runaway cow in her flight from slaughter? Why else would the owner of a slaughterhouse donate his cow to an animal sanctuary that doubled as a vegan education center?

Emily lived out the rest of her life at the Peace Abbey and died of uterine cancer at the age of ten. Her memorial service attracted international attention, and the testimonials lasted for over an hour. One testimonial in particular captured the essence of Emily's story:

> You catalyzed a new awareness in people by your very presence. One look into your large, luminous brown eyes communicated so much more than words

ever could. . . . You gave wordless testimony to the urgent necessity for an all-embracing compassion. . . . There can be no "final respects" to you, Emily, and there can be no closure until the last slaughterhouse has closed its doors, until all beings show compassion to each other, locally and globally. This is a process that will outlive me, too. Your courageous life journey will be an ongoing reminder that I must never give up. You never did.[210]

And Emily's life journey continues to be a reminder. It reminds us to refuse to allow the violent system that is carnism to blind us to the truth, the truth of the needless suffering of billions of animals—and the truth that *we care.*

Emily is immortalized by a life-sized bronze statue in her likeness that stands above her grave at the Peace Abbey. This statue, inscribed with "Emily the Sacred Cow," stands as witness to the billions of animals who are the nameless victims of carnism and to the countless humans who are fighting for their freedom. The statue of the sacred cow embodies the sacred act of bearing witness.

SEEING WITH THE HEART: THE POWER OF WITNESSING

When I last visited the Peace Abbey, I stood before each of its monuments. As I gazed up at the towering statue of Gandhi, I saw the world as he had—replete with violence and suffering, but also a place of great beauty and potential. I recalled the 1930 Salt March, and I thought of the dignity of the Indians who gave their lives in the name of nonviolent liberation. I again considered this paradox of the human experience when I looked down at the headstone-like monument inscribed "Innocent Civilians Killed in War." I envisioned the streets of Iraq, the fields of Cambodia, and the jungles of Nicaragua, littered with bodies of all shapes, sizes, colors, and ages. But, too, I remembered the 400,000 people I marched with through the frozen streets of New York City on February 15, 2003, in a peaceful demonstration against the impending invasion of Iraq. Then, as I regarded the statue of Emily, I imagined what it had been like for her, brought into this world to serve as a living machine. I thought of the dark factories, and the terror and helplessness of the countless animals within. But I also thought of the undercover investigators from the Humane Society of the United States, whose videotaping of the brutal mishandling of animals at a slaughterhouse led to public outrage and the largest beef recall in US history. At each monument, I saw the world through the eyes of those it commemorated. I became a witness.

When we bear witness, we are not merely acting as observers; we emotionally connect with the experience of those we are witnessing. We *empathize*. And in so doing, we close the gap in our consciousness, the gap that enables the violence of carnism to endure.

We discussed this gap in our consciousness in chapter 1. It is the missing link in our perception, our failure to connect meat, eggs, and dairy with their animal source. The gap blocks our disgust and our empathy. And it blocks our awareness of the incongruence between our values and our behaviors when it comes to eating animals. Witnessing closes the gap because it connects us with the truth. When we witness, we validate, or make real, the suffering the system works so hard to hide, and we also validate our authentic reaction to it. Witnessing connects us with the truth of carnistic practices, as well as with our inner truth, our empathy. We bear witness to others, and to ourselves.

Just as individual witnessing closes the gap in our consciousness, *collective witnessing* closes the gap in social consciousness. Collective witnessing leads to an informed and mobilized public and thus to a system in which values and practices are more aligned. Think about it: virtually every atrocity in the history of humankind was enabled by a populace that turned away from a reality that seemed too painful to face, while virtually every revolution for peace and justice has been made possible by a group of people who chose to bear witness and encouraged others to bear witness as well. The goal of all justice movements is to activate collective witnessing so that social practices reflect social values. A movement succeeds when it reaches a critical mass of witnesses—that is, enough witnesses to tip the scales of power in favor of the movement. Because mass witnessing is likely the single greatest threat to carnism, the entire system is organized around preventing this process. Indeed, the sole purpose of carnistic defenses is to block witnessing.

Witnessing can take many forms, including demonstrations, candlelight vigils, undercover investigations, political lobbying, and artistic creations. Witnessing has historically been a creative act: consider the revolutionary music of the 1960s; the AIDS Quilt, which spans a distance of 52.25 miles and bears over 91,000 names; the massive Vietnam Veterans' Memorial wall, which attracts three million visitors every year; the 2017 animal rights march in Israel boasting 30,000 demonstrators; and the massive actions in cities around the world organized by the Extinction Rebellion movement.

Witnessing, an act of creation, seems a natural human response to the destruction that it seeks to transform. As renowned psychiatrist Judith Herman tells us, "The ordinary response to atrocities is to banish them from consciousness. . . . Atrocities, however, refuse to be buried. Equally as powerful as the desire to deny atrocities is the conviction that denial does not work."[211] Herman goes on to say that the power of speaking the unspeakable lifts the barriers of denial and repression, releasing tremendous creative energy.

WIRED TO CARE?

Recent research suggests that there may be a biological basis for empathy. In other words, humans (as well as some other animals) may be inherently empathic. Scientists have found that our mirror neurons, neurons in our brain that fire in response to actions, can be activated whether we are performing the actions or simply witnessing them.[212] For example, seeing someone kicking a ball, crying, being harmed, or squirming with an insect crawling up their leg activates the same areas of our brain as those that would be activated if the events were happening directly to us. So, to some degree, we know what another feels not simply because we try to put ourselves in their shoes, but also because we are literally feeling the same thing.

The implications of these findings are significant. If empathy is hardwired in our brains, an automatic response, then our natural state is one of feeling for others. It may be that when we fail to empathize, we are in fact overriding a natural impulse. Carnistic defenses, then, may actually go against our nature.

FROM APATHY TO EMPATHY

All violent systems are threatened by mass witnessing because their survival depends on its opposite: mass *dissociation*. Dissociation is the core defense of carnism, the heart of psychic numbing; all other defenses support this central mechanism. Dissociation is psychologically and emotionally disconnecting from the truth of our experience; it is the feeling of not being fully "present" or conscious.

Like other mechanisms, dissociation is at times adaptive, or beneficial. For instance, when an individual is being victimized, they often automatically dissociate so as not to be overwhelmed by the stress. They may describe this sensation as feeling "spaced out" or as an "out-of-body experience." But like other mechanisms, dissociation can be *maladaptive;* it can be used to perpetuate, rather than respond to, violence. In its most extreme form, dissociation can enable a perpetrator to develop a double identity, another "self " that takes over when violating others. Psychiatrist Robert Jay Lifton discusses this phenomenon in his book *The Nazi Doctors,* where he describes medical doctors who worked as killers by day, but were able to return home to their families as seemingly normal husbands and fathers. Most of us, however, don't dissociate to the degree necessary to directly carry out killing; we simply dissociate enough to support the killing that is carried out by others. When it comes to eating animals, dissociation prevents us from connecting the dots between what we're doing and how we might actually be feeling. Dissociation essentially renders us powerless to make choices that reflect what we truly feel.

It should come as no surprise that the animals we eat aren't the only ones who pay the price for our dissociation. Dissociation limits our self-awareness and thus presents an obstacle to our personal growth. Virtually all major psychological and spiritual traditions consider self-connection, or *integration,* the goal of human development. Integration is the synthesis of different aspects of ourselves into a harmonious whole: body, mind, and spirit; id, ego, and superego; values, beliefs, and behaviors; and so on. Like dissociation, integration is not an all-or-nothing phenomenon. It exists on a spectrum. The more integrated we are, the more consistent our character is. For instance, if we're adequately integrated, we aren't a fundamentally different person in the workplace than we are at home or with our friends.

Witnessing cultivates integration, as it is an act of connecting. This happens on an individual level, as we connect to our internal experience; and also on a social level, as we connect to the experience of others. This is why witnessing is the Achilles' heel of carnism: it dispels dissociation and leads to a more integrated society. An integrated society cannot consist of people who care about animals and still support widespread animal cruelty.

WITNESSING OUR RESISTANCE

Despite the transformational power of witnessing, many people resist bearing witness to the reality of carnism. In order to overcome this resistance, we must understand its sources—we must witness our resistance.

The most obvious reason for our resistance is that the system is set up to fortify it. In chapter 5 we discussed how dominant systems shape our thoughts, feelings, and behaviors by laying out invisible "paths of least resistance" for us to follow. These paths dictate the "normal" way to be, which is believing and acting in accordance with the tenets of the system. Dominant systems maintain their dominance by coercing us to conform to the norm. To witness is to deviate from the path of least resistance.

Another reason we may resist bearing witness to the truth of carnism is that witnessing hurts. Becoming aware of the intense suffering of billions of animals, and of our own participation in that suffering, can bring up painful emotions: sorrow and grief for the animals; anger at the injustice and deception of the system; despair at the enormity of the problem; fear that trusted authorities and institutions are, in fact, untrustworthy; and guilt for having contributed to the problem. Bearing witness means choosing to feel pain. Indeed, empathy is literally "feeling with." Choosing to feel pain is particularly difficult in a culture that is addicted to comfort—a culture that teaches us that pain should be avoided whenever possible and that ignorance is bliss. We can reduce our resistance to witnessing by valuing authenticity over personal pleasure, and integration over ignorance.

A related reason we may resist witnessing the truth of carnism is that we feel powerless to change suffering of such magnitude. It is all too easy to feel discouraged if we believe that "fixing" a problem means that change must be immediate and total. It's important to accept that change—especially significant change—is a process. And in fact the very act of witnessing is an act of empowerment; it effects immediate change in ourselves, by integrating our values and practices. As vegan advocate Eddie Lama points out, "I realize that animals will continue to suffer and die—but not because of *me*." [213]

There's a final, perhaps more fundamental, reason we may resist witnessing the truth of carnism: if we no longer feel entitled to kill and consume animals, our identity as human beings comes into question. Witnessing compels us to view ourselves as strands in the web of life, rather than as standing at the apex of the so-called food chain. Witnessing challenges our sense of human superiority; it forces us to acknowledge our interconnectedness with the rest of the natural world, an interconnectedness our species has made every effort to deny for thousands of years. And yet witnessing is ultimately liberating. When we recognize that we aren't isolated fragments in a disconnected world, but rather are a part of a vast, living collective, we connect with a power much greater than our individual selves. We no longer support a system that is based on domination and subjugation, a system that follows Hitler's credo that "he who does not possess power loses the right to life."[214] We learn, as author Matthew Scully says, not to measure our lives "in things appropriated, crushed, and killed."[215]

The paradox is that the very reason we resist bearing witness to the truth of carnism is the same reason we desire to witness: because we *care*. This is the great truth that lies buried beneath the elaborate, labyrinthine mechanisms of the system. Because we care, we want to turn away. And because we care, we feel compelled to bear witness. The way to overcome this paradox is to integrate our witnessing: *we must witness the truth of carnism while witnessing ourselves.* We must extend to ourselves the same compassion we allow ourselves to feel for the animals. When we compassionately witness ourselves, we witness our feelings, but without judgment. We recognize ourselves as victims in a system that has led us down the path of least resistance. But we also recognize that we have the power to choose a different path: we have the opportunity to make our choices freely, without the psychological constraints of a covert and coercive system.

WITNESSING THE ZEITGEIST

Despite the extensive reach of carnism, there is reason to believe that the system will destabilize, and the timing is ripe to push for transformation. There are several reasons that challenging carnism is timely: an increased awareness of the environmental crisis; a growing concern with animal protection; the increasing credibility and popularity of veganism; and the unprecedented availability of information on both carnism and veganism.

As noted in chapters 3 and 4, animal agriculture is a leading cause of environmental destruction, including climate change.[216] Methane gasses emitted from thousands of pounds of manure deplete the ozone layer. Toxic runoff from tons of chemicals used on the animals—synthetic hormones, antibiotics, pesticides, and fungicides—pollute the air and waterways. Thousands of acres of woodlands are clear-cut to allow for the planting of feed crops, leading to topsoil erosion and deforestation. More fresh water is usurped from reservoirs than can be replenished. And chemical fertilizers seep into rivers and streams, enabling the proliferation of microorganisms that destroy aquatic life. Leading scientists agree that the system of mass carnistic production cannot continue without causing a breakdown of the ecosystem. Environmental protection has become an increasingly important concern, as can be seen through the proliferation of "green" products, publications, and policies. As people become more concerned about ecological sustainability, they invariably become more concerned about carnistic practices.

Perhaps not coincidentally, people have also become more concerned with farmed animal protection and more open to veganism. This is demonstrated by the countless farmed animal protection and vegan advocacy organizations that have sprung up across the country and around the world; the massive growth in the vegan food industry (In 2018, the global vegan food market size was valued at $12.69 billion, and it is projected to expand at a compound annual growth rate of 9.6 percent between 2019 and 2025)[217] and the proliferation of vegan-focused books and films, such as the James Cameron hit *The Game Changers*.

Veganism, once considered an extreme ideology and a diet of questionable nutritional soundness, is making its way into the mainstream. While vegans still make up a minority of the population, and many health professionals still cling to carnistic myths, individuals who eschew carnistic products are far less marginalized and pathologized than they were just five years ago. The face of veganism is no longer the flower child of the 1960s; celebrities from Moby and Miley Cyrus to Bill Pearl, bodybuilder and five-time Mr. Universe, are ambassadors for a diverse, growing movement. And more and more studies have compelled the medical community to admit that not only can a plant-based diet be as healthful as an animal-based one, but there's a good chance it's even healthier. Indeed, the proliferation of vegan publications, food products, restaurants, and organizations indicates that the vegan movement is rapidly increasing in size and strength.

A final reason that the timing is ripe to challenge carnism is that the primary defense of the system, invisibility, has been weakening. It is becoming increasingly difficult for carnistic industries to hide their secrets from the public; the animal agribusinesses that depend on controlling information to sustain the myths of carnism have been consistently challenged by a ubiquitous, unregulated information source: the Internet. Carnism is like the Wizard of Oz: once the curtain is pulled back from the system, its power virtually disappears.

> **Threats Are REAL**
> **Threats Are NOW**
> **Potential Impact Is Enormous**
>
> —Slide at the end of a PowerPoint presentation entitled *Animal Welfare and Activism: What You Need to Know,* from the 2008 Food Marketing Institute/ American Meat Institute Meat Conference

WITNESSING IN ACTION:
WHAT YOU CAN DO

As I mentioned earlier, witnessing the extensive suffering inherent in carnism can cause one to feel helpless and frustrated. But there *are* things you can do that will directly impact your own life and the lives of farmed animals and the environment.

There are three important steps you can take to get started: commit to making each meal as vegan as possible, support a vegan advocacy organization, and continue to inform yourself and others. In short, be a *vegan ally*—use your influence to support veganism and vegans even if you are not yet fully vegan yourself.

Although eliminating your consumption of carnistic products is a goal to work toward, reducing the amount of them in your diet as you transition from carnism can nevertheless have a significant impact on animals, the environment, and yourself; for instance, a person who eats carnistic products once or twice a month consumes far fewer animals than someone who eats such products daily. Clearly, this helps animals and reduces your carbon footprint. But you, too, benefit, as you feel more integrated in your values and practices and likely reap substantial health benefits.

And you don't need to work toward change on your own. Millions of people around the world are actively working to transform carnism, and it's easier than ever to join up with or otherwise support them. If a vegan group or organization doesn't exist in your region, you can connect with one online. Getting involved with an organization gives you options for contributing to the cause. You can donate money, help with advocacy efforts, or do any number of things to be a part of the solution. (You can find more suggestions as well as resources at *carnism.org*.)

And finally, you can and should continue to learn and educate others. It's all too easy to forget, to fall back into the cocoon of carnistic numbing. Remember: your carnistic schema will pull you back into the carnistic mentality; your awareness of carnistic production will likely diminish if you don't actively work to keep yourself informed and try to deepen your understanding of the issue.* Make witnessing your credo.

BEYOND CARNISM

The mechanisms that enable widescale carnistic consumption are not unique to carnism. As I have pointed out, carnism is just one of numerous violent ideologies, or oppressive systems.** And any ideology that requires the participation of individuals who, if they were more fully informed, might choose to withhold their support utilizes the same mechanisms as carnism. Thus, understanding carnism can help us think more critically about all systems in which we participate. Consider the arguments and psychology that have enabled widespread hatred and discrimination toward members of the LGBTQ+ community, the deeply entrenched system of apartheid, and the genocide in Darfur. In each of these instances, the violence has been denied, justified, and distorted to garner mass support.

The same holds true for witnessing: because violent systems share similar structural features, witnessing carnism can give us a framework for witnessing other systems. Indeed, the ability to witness extends beyond carnism because witnessing isn't merely something one *does*; it is how one *is*. Witnessing isn't an isolated practice, but a way of relating to oneself and the world. It is a way of life that informs our interactions

---

* Staying informed does *not* mean continually exposing yourself to graphic imagery of animal exploitation. Once you're aware of the suffering of farmed animals, you don't need to expose yourself to potentially traumatizing information.
** I've recently published a book on this subject, entitled *Powerarchy: Understanding the Psychology of Oppression for Social Transformation*.

with ourselves and others. And there is no limit to our capacity for witnessing.* In fact, because witnessing is empowering, the more we witness, the greater our ability to witness. Like compassion, our capacity for witnessing grows with practice.

THE COURAGE TO WITNESS

Bearing witness takes courage. It takes courage to open our hearts to the suffering of others and to acknowledge that, for better or worse, we are part of the system in which that suffering takes place. Indeed, as James O'Dea, former director of Amnesty International, explains:

> The witness stands together, inside, with those who are hurt and with those who are violated; the witness has an extraordinary capacity to stand in the fires of hatred and violence without increasing those elements. In fact, the deepest form of witnessing is a form of compassion for all suffering beings. . . . In reality, we are never outside observers. We are inside the wound together. It is just that some feel and some are numb. We are inside the very thing that needs to be transformed.[218]

Bearing witness takes the courage to refuse to follow the path of least resistance. Like Emily the cow, we have been herded into a lineup, taught to follow a course that's been laid out for us. But like Emily, we can choose to break from the line and shift the trajectory of our lives. Whether or not you were previously aware of the truth of carnism, that you have chosen to read this book is testament to your courage to take the road

---

* Though witnessing may at times be painful, it should never make you feel emotionally unsafe. Witnessing means staying mentally and emotionally open to the experience of oneself and others; it does not mean forcing yourself to take in deeply distressing information. Many animal advocates become traumatized from overexposing themselves to the horrors of carnistic production—this kind of witnessing is unnecessary and is ultimately counterproductive.

less traveled. The information in this book is provocative, challenging, and at times disturbing, and it takes courage to witness it.

Bearing witness takes the courage to realize the potential of the human spirit. Witnessing requires us to call forth the highest qualities of our species, qualities such as conviction, integrity, empathy, and compassion. It is easier by far to retain the attributes of carnistic culture: apathy, complacency, self-interest, and "blissful" ignorance. I wrote this book—itself an act of witnessing—because I believe that, as humans, we have a fundamental desire to strive to become our best selves. I believe that virtually all of us have the capacity to act as powerful witnesses in a world very much in need. I have had the opportunity to interact with thousands of individuals through my work as a teacher, author, and speaker, and through my personal life. I have witnessed, again and again, the courage and compassion of the so-called average person: previously apathetic students who become impassioned activists; lifelong meat eaters who weep openly when exposed to images of carnistic production, never again to eat animals; butchers who suddenly connect meat to its living source and become unable to continue killing animals; and a community of meat eaters who aid a runaway cow in her flight from slaughter.

Ultimately, bearing witness requires the courage to choose a role. Judith Herman points out that, in the face of mass violence, all bystanders are forced to take a side, by their action or inaction, and that there is no such thing as moral neutrality. Indeed, as Nobel Peace Prize Laureate and Holocaust survivor Elie Wiesel stated, "Neutrality helps the oppressor, never the victim. Silence encourages the tormentor, never the tormented."[219] Witnessing enables us to choose our role rather than have one assigned to us. And although those of us who choose to stand with the victim may feel some emotional pain, as Herman says, "There can be no greater honor."[220]

Afterword

It has been ten years since *Why We Love Dogs* was first published, and it is a privilege to contribute to this new edition and reflect on the events and ideas that the book helped catalyze.

A VERY BRIEF SUMMARY OF THE POST—WHY WE LOVE DOGS DECADE

At present, *Why We Love Dogs* has been published or is in print in 17 languages—some editions of which are bestselling and award-winning—and it is considered a seminal work in the canon of animal rights literature. Its publication in 2010 led me to begin what became a global speaking tour, spanning six continents and about fifty countries and attracting widespread media attention, from the BBC to ABC Australia. Moreover, *Why We Love Dogs* played a role in me receiving several important awards, including the Ahimsa Award, which was previously given to Nelson Mandela and the Dalai Lama.

The book also laid the foundation for my organization, Beyond Carnism, an international NGO whose mission is to expose and transform carnism globally. One of our key programs is the Center for Effective Advocacy (CEA), which is headed by vegan strategist Tobias Leenaert and me, and whose current purpose is to increase the impact of vegan advocacy worldwide. Tobias and I travel extensively, giving trainings and providing other forms of support to vegan advocates around the world.

Why We Love Dogs paved the way as well for me to cofound ProVeg International, a food-awareness NGO headquartered in Berlin, Germany, where I eventually moved to work alongside (and marry) its founding CEO, Sebastian Joy. ProVeg's mission is to reduce global animal consumption by 50 percent by 2040.

Others, too, have used *Why We Love Dogs* as a platform with which to examine and challenge carnistic psychology and ideology. For example, a number of social scientists have built on and empirically tested my theory of carnism, developing instruments to assess its validity and to understand carnism as a form of prejudice.

Why We Love Dogs not only helped launch a global network of advocates and allies, but it also laid the groundwork for me to develop new ideas that built on, deepened, and broadened my original analysis.

EXPANDING THE THEORY OF CARNISM: NEOCARNISM AND SECONDARY CARNISTIC DEFENSES

Shortly after the release of *Why We Love Dogs*, I began expanding my theory of carnism. Two such expansions emerged from my realization that, as awareness of the injustice of animal agriculture was growing, so, too, was the backlash against veganism.

In 2012, I published an article about what I called neocarnism, new forms of carnism that emerged as part of the "carnistic backlash," serving to bolster a system that had been increasingly challenged. There are three main manifestations of neocarnism, each providing a carnistic justification meant to weaken one of the three main arguments for veganism: animal welfare, environmental protection, and human health. Each neocarnism also bolsters one of the Three Ns of Justification—eating animals is normal, natural, and necessary—and thus also promotes the myths that *not* eating animals is *ab*normal, *un*natural, and *un*necessary.

The neocarnism I call "compassionate carnism" is expressed through the belief that it is possible to procure "humane" meat, eggs, and dairy; and this form of neocarnism reflects a backlash against the animal welfare argument for veganism. If farmed animal welfare were truly a possibility (which it is not, given the current system, and which it never could be, given that the very existence of farmed animals is itself antithetical to their welfare—farmed animals have been created by and for humans and are by definition exploited), then veganism wouldn't be needed. Compassionate carnism bolsters the myths that eating animals is normal and not eating animals is abnormal. Veganism, presented by animal agribusinesses and other institutions as extreme and radical, is juxtaposed with "humane" meat, eggs, and dairy, making compassionate carnism seem like a mainstream (normal) alternative to both extremes: the brutality of factory farming and the seemingly radical practice of veganism. In other words, carnistic consumers can stay within the carnistic norm while assuaging their conscience by believing that they are eating animals who were supposedly treated kindly.

The neocarnism I call "ecocarnism" is expressed largely through the locavore and, to some degree, foodie movements. Ecocarnism frames hunting and raising one's own animals for slaughter as natural and healthful, while framing veganism as a trend, an aberration of modern life. Vegans are portrayed as hypersensitive, squeamish urbanites and suburbanites who are removed from the true source of their food and thus disconnected from reality.

Ecocarnism bolsters the myths that eating animals is natural and not eating animals is unnatural. Proponents of ecocarnism argue that in order to live and eat healthfully, we need to get back to nature—our human nature, and the natural world—which includes transcending our reluctance to get our hands dirty by tilling land and killing animals. Ecocarnsim glorifies our omnivorous history, whereby we were much less removed from and seemingly more comfortable with slaughtering animals. One must remember that, in previous eras, we were also less removed from and more comfortable with killing humans—consider the Roman games and public executions—but we're not encouraged to re-adopt these behaviors today because we realize that empathy and compassion are qualities we should strive to cultivate, rather than transcend.

Finally, the neocarnism I call "biocarnism" is a manifestation of the backlash against the health argument for veganism. This neocarnism can be seen through such fads as the Paleo or Keto diet, and it upholds the myths that eating animals is necessary and not eating animals is unnecessary.

Analyzing the carnistic backlash also led me to recognize that there was not one, but two, types of carnistic defenses, and in 2013 I wrote an article about this phenomenon. I realized that carnism (and, by extension, other oppressive systems) can only persist if it remains stronger than the counter-system that challenges it, and that carnistic defenses therefore needed to achieve two ends: they needed to both validate carnism and invalidate veganism. I refer to the defenses that serve the former end as "primary defenses" and those that serve the latter end as "secondary defenses."

Secondary defenses invalidate veganism in three ways: through invalidating vegan ideology, the vegan movement, and vegans. Secondary defenses invalidate vegan ideology by suggesting that, for example, veganism is abnormal, unnatural, and unnecessary. They invalidate the vegan movement by, for instance, suggesting that there *is* no movement (that veganism is just a "trend"). And they invalidate vegans in large part through promulgating inaccurate, negative stereotypes that cause meat eaters—or *nonvegans*—to feel defensive against the information vegans share: if we shoot the messenger, we don't have to take seriously the implications of their message. For example, vegans are often portrayed as overly emotional, animal-loving sentimentalists. If someone is overly emotional, by definition they are not rational, and people who are not rational are not worth listening to. (Of course, sadness and anger are legitimate, healthful responses to the atrocity that is carnism; much more concerning is the epidemic apathy that is an inevitable consequence of widespread carnistic zombification.) Unfortunately, there is a long list of anti-vegan stereotypes that cause people to resist the very information that would free them from the carnistic box they don't even realize they're in, and secondary defenses work to ensure that such stereotypes remain intact.

BEYOND CARNISM: RELATIONAL LITERACY AND POWERARCHY

During my talks and trainings, I started to notice a pattern that concerned me. A number of vegan attendees were sharing similar stories: after becoming vegan, their relationships and communications with nonvegans had started to break down. These stories were also the subject of countless emails and Facebook messages I'd been receiving. Clearly, vegans (and sometimes vegetarians and even meat eaters who interacted with vegetarians or vegans) needed advice on how to navigate their inter-ideological relationships and dialogues, which had become fraught with problems.

I felt personally saddened by these stories, as well as by the irony that we live in a world where choosing to practice integrity so often comes at the price of losing people we love. I also felt frustrated; I had worked as a relationship coach for a number of years and I knew that much of the suffering I was witnessing was preventable and reversible with the right tools.

I came to realize that relationship and communication breakdown was taking a tremendous toll on vegans, and, therefore, on the vegan movement as a whole. Indeed, research has shown that people in connected, fulfilling relationships fare better in pretty much all areas of life: they live longer, they're healthier, they're happier, and they have greater career success—so I imagined the impact on vegans of not only the *absence* of such relationships, but of the *presence* of disrupted ones. A massive amount of energy was being siphoned out of a movement that needed all the help it could get.

It had been seven years since the publication of *Why We Love Dogs*, and I'd promised myself that that would be my last book. But I was uniquely positioned to write on the subject of relationships and communication among vegans and nonvegans, since I was a psychologist, relationship coach, and long-time vegan advocate. So, I poured myself into writing a new book, doing a deep dive into all the relevant research I could find and then parsing and analyzing what seemed like a massive amount of information, eventually synthesizing it with my own theories and insights. The result was *Beyond Beliefs: A Guide to Improving Relationships and Communication Among Vegans, Vegetarians, and Meat Eaters*.

In the book, I present a concept I refer to as "relationship resilience," a blueprint for healthy relationships, and tailor this approach specifically for people in relationships involving at least one vegan (or vegetarian). I discuss such ideas as how carnism is an invisible intruder in "veg/non-veg" relationships, triangulating them and distorting both parties' perceptions; and how the traumatization that many vegans experience from witnessing animal suffering can cause them to unconsciously disconnect from both nonvegans and other vegans.

Writing *Beyond Beliefs* unleashed a plethora of pent-up thoughts, triggering a process of analysis that generated new ideas, which then warranted writing new books. So, after years of virtually no writing, I suddenly found myself unable to stop.

I had included a chapter in *Beyond Beliefs* that touched on a new theory I had been developing about relational power dynamics and the psychology of oppression. The chapter turned out not to be a fit for the book so I decided to cut it. Eventually, this chapter evolved into its own book: *Powerarchy: Understanding the Psychology of Oppression for Social Transformation.*

In *Powerarchy*, I propose that oppression (and also abuse, which is essentially oppression on a smaller scale and that's not institutionalized) reflects and reinforces relational dysfunction, a dysfunction in how we relate: as social groups, as individuals to other human and nonhuman beings and to the environment, and even to ourselves. All oppressive and abusive systems (such as sexism, carnism, or an abusive relationship) reflect the same essential mentality and share the same basic structure: they are all relationally dysfunctional, or *nonrelational*, systems. Nonrelational systems are based on the belief in a hierarchy of moral worth—that some individuals or groups are more worthy of moral consideration than others—and they are structured to create and maintain unjust power imbalances. Such systems condition us to think and act in ways that are antithetical to healthy relating: they teach us to violate our integrity (we don't practice justice and compassion) and harm the dignity of others, resulting in disconnection between ourselves and others and also within ourselves. If we imagine oppressions as spokes on a wheel, powerarchy is the hub. It is the *metasystem* of oppression.

In *Powerarchy*, I deconstruct the system, outlining its defensive structure in a similar way as I did in *Why We Love Dogs* but incorporating more features and analyses. I also suggest tools for transformation, most notably developing what I call *relational literacy*—the understanding of and ability to practice healthy ways of relating—which is the focus of the next book I wrote.

I had always envisioned reworking the manuscript that became *Beyond Beliefs* it into a book for a mainstream audience, because relational dysfunction affects everyone, and the suffering it causes is largely preventable and treatable with the right understanding and tools. Having coached countless people struggling with their romantic relationships, family dynamics, and leadership, I had long wished for a book I could point them to that covered all the relevant approaches to relational health—a "one-stop guide" that also included a focus on how systems of oppression inevitably yet profoundly impact relationships. And, during my deep dive into research and theorizing for *Beyond Beliefs* and *Powerarchy*, I had come to realize the essential role that developing relational literacy plays in cultivating genuine and lasting social transformation. Indeed, were our collective level of relational literacy not so low—were we not living in the relational Dark Ages—we would no doubt recognize toxic, nonrelational leaders, policies, and practices for what they are and withhold our support from them. The world would be a profoundly different place.

The good news is that the very principles and tools which inform healthy interpersonal relationships inform all kinds of relationships. So, people who learn how to improve their interpersonal relationships are invariably more able—and likely—to improve the way they relate all around. In other words, when someone learns to be more mindful, self-aware, empathic, and committed to practicing integrity toward family, friends, and colleagues (and they understand the ways systems of oppression condition them to disconnect from their authentic thoughts and feelings), they are better positioned to treat others, including other animals, more respectfully and to help create a more compassionate world for all beings. My book *Getting Relationships Right: How to Build Resilience and Thrive in Life, Love, and Work* aims to help foster both personal and social transformation, to support holistic and lasting change through promoting relational literacy.

The fourth book to be published post—*Why We Love Dogs . . .* is a short text about how powerarchy, and specifically the dynamics of privilege and oppression it creates, operates within the vegan movement. It's entitled *The Vegan Matrix: Understanding and Discussing Privilege Among Vegans to Build a More Inclusive and Empowered Movement* and it started as a series of essays I wrote shortly after the #ARMeToo* uprising. I wrote *The Vegan Matrix* to help address the problem of unexamined privilege among vegans and to provide guidelines for how to talk about privilege when either ours is being challenged or we're challenging the privilege of others.

I had long known that unexamined sexism, racism, classism, and other powerarchies were creating interpersonal problems among vegans as well as between vegans and those who might otherwise be allies to the movement, such as feminists and social justice advocates. But I didn't have the capacity to take on another writing project. However, I eventually realized the extent of the damage this issue was causing. I also realized that, although there were some excellent materials on the subject of privilege and oppression among vegans, these materials often didn't speak to people who weren't already relatively well informed about the issue. Moreover, the post-#ARMeToo conversation that was unfolding was in some ways creating more problems than it was resolving; communication was breaking down and divisions among vegans were growing.

In *The Vegan Matrix*, I use carnistic privilege in juxtaposition with other forms of privilege to create a familiar point of entry for vegan readers who wish to learn about privilege and oppression in the movement (and beyond). The book also includes suggestions for how to discuss unexamined privilege

---

* #ARMeToo is the animal rights version of #MeToo.

so that the dialogue doesn't lead to gridlock. The goal of the book is to help unify vegans to create a more empowered movement and therefore a more effective and impactful force for animals. The goal of the book is also to reduce injustice and suffering beyond the vegan movement.

Why We Love Dogs started a process that continues to unfold in ways I could never have imagined and that has taken on a life of its own. I feel hopeful, heartened, and curious as to what the future will bring. I will continue to work to expose and transform carnism; to empower those on the frontlines of the vegan movement; to raise awareness of powerarchy more broadly; and to promote relational literacy as a key tool for transformation.

I have little doubt that one day, veganism will replace carnism as the dominant ideology. The question, to me, is not *whether*, but *when*. Indeed, I never imagined I'd live to see the blossoming of the vegan movement that's currently unfolding—the increasing numbers of vegans, vegan organizations and establishments, and vegan allies around the world. Even though in some places carnistic consumption is increasing (Big Agribusiness is following in the footsteps of Big Tobacco and exporting its problems to countries that are more vulnerable to its toxic influence) and farmed animal exploitation is indeed still a global catastrophe, the vegan movement is mushrooming. I do believe that we are on the cusp of a revolution—one which will forever transform humanity and the world as we know it—and I feel honored and humbled to have been able to play a small part in this deeply inspiring process.

Book Group Discussion Guide

CHAPTER 1. TO LOVE OR TO EAT?

- People tend to have different levels of tolerance for eating "unusual" types or cuts of meat. For instance, some meat eaters avoid cuts that are atypical (e.g., turkey necks), while others are more "adventurous" and willing to try different types of meat. Why do you think this is, and how can understanding these differences influence how one discusses the ethics of eating animals?

- Why, exactly, is empathy "integral to our sense of self," and how might blocking our empathy toward certain species impact our capacity for empathy in general?

- Before reading the dinner party scene in the opening of the book, had you ever wondered why you eat some animals but not others? If not, why not? If so, when and why?

- Was there ever a time in your life when you felt uncomfortable eating "normal" types and cuts of meat? Why? How did you react to this discomfort?

- Was there ever a time in your life when you had a negative impression of vegetarians or vegans? What was your impression, and why do you think you had it?

CHAPTER 2. CARNISM: "IT'S JUST THE WAY THINGS ARE"

- Speciesism is the ideology in which it's considered appropriate to value some animals over others. How does speciesism inform carnism? What are the similarities and differences between these ideologies?

- Is carnism the "opposite" of vegetarianism, or veganism?

- Feminists have been successful in their attempts to challenge sexism not by arguing that everybody should become a feminist, but by highlighting the ideology of patriarchy—the ideology that enables sexism. Most people don't support sexism but also don't consider themselves feminists. How might those who wish to challenge carnism use a similar approach?

- Carnism reframes eating animals so that this practice is seen not simply as a matter of personal ethics, but as the inevitable end result of a deeply entrenched belief system. How might this reframe help eating animals become recognized as a social justice issue, and what implications does this have for vegan advocacy?

CHAPTER 3. THE WAY THINGS REALLY ARE

- This chapter focuses on the abuse inherent in factory farms, or CAFOs, which is where the majority of carnistic products are produced. Do you think the concept of carnism applies to smaller family farms? Why or why not?

- This chapter can be difficult to read, as it gives graphic descriptions of animal suffering. How did reading this chapter affect you? What was most interesting or shocking about it?

CHAPTER 4. COLLATERAL DAMAGE

- This chapter describes the consequences of carnism on humans and the environment. How might those concerned with animal protection use the concept of carnism to reach out to or ally themselves with those working for human rights and environmental justice?

- Animal agribusiness lobbies play a major role in maintaining the economic and legislative power of carnistic industry, just as tobacco lobbies have done for the tobacco industry. How might framing eating animals as an ideologically driven behavior help challenge lobbyists and the legislation or other support they push for, such as meat, egg, and dairy subsidies?

- "Routinization" is common among those who work in the meatpacking industry. Do you think routinization plays a role in carnistic consumers' experience as well?

CHAPTER 5. THE MYTHOLOGY
OF EATING ANIMALS

- The locavore movement, heralded by those such as Michael Pollan (*The Omnivore's Dilemma*), opposes factory farming but supports and even celebrates the killing and consumption of (certain) animals. Pollan, for instance, has said that hunting is an expression of the natural order of life: ". . . man had done nothing to create this food chain, only stepped into a role prepared long ago for the Predator" (362–3). He also says that the moral ambivalence of the hunter is what makes hunting commendable (361). How does the concept of carnism apply to the locavore movement? Which of the Three Ns (eating meat is *n*ormal, *n*atural, and *n*ecessary) are most relied upon to support "ecocarnism"?*

- Do you believe it's ethical to consume meat, eggs, or dairy from animals raised on small-scale farms? Why or why not?

- Michael Pollan also has said that, though part of him envies the moral consistency of the vegetarian, part of him pities vegetarians because "dreams of innocence are just that; they usually depend on a denial of reality that can be its own form of hubris" (362). How might this comment be interpreted through the lens of carnism?

- Different people are affected by the Ns differently; some people are more influenced by one N than others. How might understanding this point support vegan outreach? Which Ns have influenced you most?

- A common carnistic justification, not mentioned in this book, is the argument that if plants are sentient (as some research is believed to suggest), then eating animals is no different from eating plants. How might the "plants suffer, too" argument be used to bolster carnism, and how can one respond to this justification?

- Since it takes vastly more plant life to feed the animals who are then consumed by humans than it would were humans to eat the plants directly, could one argue that carnism harms more plants than necessary, to sustain human consumers?

---

* For an explanation of ecocarnism, see the Afterword.

CHAPTER 6. THROUGH THE CARNISTIC LOOKING GLASS

- Do ovo-lacto vegetarians, who consume dairy products from certain animals and the eggs of certain birds, use carnistic numbing? How and why?

- Do you feel you have stepped outside of the carnistic matrix? If so, what induced this? Was it a single event, or a series of events? If you have not, why not?

CHAPTER 7. BEARING WITNESS

- Witnessing is the cornerstone of social justice. What are some concrete actions that witnesses can carry out to help bring about justice for animals and other victims of oppressive systems?

- Overwitnessing is a common experience among those working for social change, and it can lead to traumatization and burnout. What are some ways people can be active witnesses without burning out?

- How can we create an atmosphere that helps others move toward a state of readiness to bear witness?

Endnotes

1 Victor Benno Meyer-Rochow, "Food Taboos: Their Origins and Purposes," *Journal of Ethnobiology and Ethnomedicine* 8 (2009): 18, https://doi.org; Daniel M. T. Fessler and Carlos David Navarrete, "Meat Is Good to Taboo," *Journal of Cognition and Culture* (2003), http://cognitionandculture.net.

2 Nida Najar and Suhasini Raj, "Indian State Is Expanding Penalty for Killing a Cow to Life in Prison," *New York Times*, March 31, 2017, https://www.nytimes.com; Krishnadev Calamur, "India's Food Fight Turns Deadly," *Atlantic*, October 8, 2015, https://www.theatlantic.com; Supriya Nair, "The Meaning of India's 'Beef Lynchings,'" *Atlantic*, July 24, 2017, https://www.theatlantic.com; Anna Collinson, "Why the UK Doesn't Eat Dog Meat, but People in China Do," *Newsbeat*, http://www.bbc.co.uk/newsbeat; Telegraph Reporters, "EDL Protesters Holding Pig's Head in Anti-Muslim Slur Clash with Police at Counter-Terror March in Manchester," *Telegraph*, June 12, 2017, https://www.telegraph.co.uk; "Seoul: Anti-Dog Meat Protestors Facing Provocative Dog Meat Consumers," *EuroNews*, July 12, 2019, https://www.euronews.com.

3 Lotte Holm and M. Mohl, "The Role of Meat in Everyday Food Culture: An Analysis of an Interview Study in Copenhagen," *Appetite* 34 (2000): 277–83.

4 Nick Fiddes, *Meat: A Natural Symbol* (New York: Rutledge, 1991); Peter Farb and George Armelagos, *Consuming Passions: The Anthropology of Eating* (Boston: Houghton Mifflin, 1980); Frederick J. Simoons, *Eat Not This Flesh: Food Avoidances in the Old World* (Madison: University of Wisconsin Press, 1961); "Food Taboos: It's All a Matter of Taste," *National Geographic News*, https://www.nationalgeographic.com; Daniel Fessler, M. T. Navarrette, and Carlos David Navarrette, "Meat Is Good to Taboo: Dietary Proscriptions as a Product of the Interaction of Psychological Mechanisms and Social Processes," *Journal of Cognition and Culture* 3.1 (2003): 1–40, semanticscholar.org.

5 Farb and Armelagos, *Consuming Passions*; Simoons, *Eat Not This Flesh*; Daniel Kelly, "The Role of Psychology in the Study of Culture," *Purdue University*, http://web.ics.purdue.edu.

6 Zeiad Amjad Aghwan and Joe Mac Regenstein, "Slaughter Practices of Different Faiths in Different Countries," *Journal of Animal Science and Technology* 61, no. 3 (2019): 111-21, https://www.ncbi.nlm.nih.gov; E. Szűcs, R. Geers, T. Jezierski, E. N. Sossidou, and D. M. Broom, "Animal Welfare in Different Human Cultures, Traditions and Religious Faiths," *Asian-Australasian Journal of Animal Sciences* 25, no. 11 (2012): 1499–1506,

https://www.ncbi.nlm.nih.gov; "Vegetarianism," *Encyclopedia Britannica*, n.d., https://www.britannica.com; Gunnel Ekroth, "Meat in Ancient Greece: Sacrificial, Sacred or Secular?," *Food & History* 5, no. 1 (2007): 249–72, https://www.academia.edu.

7   Harish, "How Many Animals Does a Vegetarian Save?," *Counting Animals*, March 16, 2015, http://www.countinganimals.com.

8   Cited in Dave Grossman, *On Killing: The Psychological Cost of Learning to Kill in War and Society* (New York: Back Bay Books, 1996).

9   Grossman, *On Killing*, 12.

10 Grossman, *On Killing*; Martha Stout, *The Sociopath Next Door* (New York: Broadway Books, 2005).

11 Grossman, *On Killing*, 15.

12 National Agriculture Statistics Service, *Poultry—Production and Value, 2018 Summary* (Washington, DC: USDA, 2019), https://www.nass.usda.gov.

13 National Agriculture Statistics Service, *Poultry—Production and Value*.

14 M. Shahbandeh, "Per Capita Consumption of Beef in the U.S. 2000–2028," *Statista*, March 14, 2019, https://www.statista.com.

15 US Department of Agriculture, "Per Capita Availability of Chicken Higher Than That of Beef," August 28, 2019, https://www.ers.usda.gov.

16 National Agriculture Statistics Service, Poultry—*Production and Value;* M. Shahbandeh, "Per Capita Consumption of Beef in the U.S."; US Department of Agriculture, "Per Capita Availability of Chicken Higher Than That of Beef"; Megan Durisin and Shruti Singh, "Americans Will Eat a Record Amount of Meat in 2018," *Bloomberg*, January 2, 2018, https://www.bloomberg.com.

17 US Department of Agriculture, "Food Availability (Per Capita) Data System," n.d., https://www.ers.usda.gov./

18 Food and Agriculture Organization of the United States, "Food Supply—Livestock and Fish Primary Equivalent," n.d., http://www.fao.org.

19 US Department of Agriculture, "Livestock & Meat Domestic Data," n.d., https://www.ers.usda.gov.

20 Harish, "How Many Animals Does a Vegetarian Save?"

21 US Department of Agriculture, "Cattle/Calves Accounted for Nearly 40 Percent of 2018 U.S. Animal/Product Receipts," n.d., https://www.ers.usda.gov.

22 Eurostat, *Agriculture, Forestry, and Fishery Statistics* (Luxembourg: Eurostat, 2018), https://ec.europa.eu/eurostat/; US Department of Agriculture, "Cattle/Calves Accounted for Nearly 40 Percent."

23 Natural Resources Conservation Service, "Animal Feeding Operations," n.d., https://www.nrcs.usda.gov.

24 Health for Animals, "Global Challenges: Animal Disease," n.d., https://healthforanimals.org.

25 Daniel Zwerdling, "A View to a Kill," *Gourmet* (June 2007), http://www.gourmet.com. Also see Kim Severson, "Upton Sinclair, Now Playing on You Tube," *New York Times*, March 12, 2008, http://www.nytimes.com.

26 Eric Schlosser, "Fast Food Nation: Meat and Potatoes," *Rolling Stone*, September 3, 1998, www.rollingstone.com.

27 Center for Constitutional Rights, *Ag-Gag Across America: Corporate Backed Attacks on Activists and Whistleblowers* (New York: Center for Constitutional Rights and Defending Rights & Dissent, 2017), https://ccrjustice.org; ASPCA, "What Is Ag-Gag Legislation?," n.d., https://www.aspca.org; ACLU, "ACLU Letter to Congress Urging Opposition to the Animal Enterprise Act, S. 1926 and H.R. 4239," n.d., https://www.aclu.org.

28 Study cited by the Humane Society of the United States, available at http://www.hsus.org.

29 Lori Marino and Christina M. Colvin, "Thinking Pigs: A Comparative Review of Cognition, Emotion, and Personality in *Sus domesticus*," *International Journal of Comparative Psychology* 28 (2015): 1–22, escholarship.org; Anna K. Johnson and Jeremy N. Marchant-Forde, "Natural Farrowing Behavior of the Sow and Piglets," Pork Information Gateway, December 29, 2010, http://porkgateway.org.

30 Jim Barrett, "United States Hog Inventory Up 4 Percent," US Department of Agriculture, June 27, 2019, https://www.nass.usda.gov.

31 American Veterinary Medical Association, "Tail Docking and Teeth Clipping of Swine," n.d., https://www.avma.org.

32 Yuzhi Lee, Lee Johnston, and Wayne Martin, "Docking the Tail or Not: Effect on Tail Damage, Skin Lesions and Growth Performance in Growing-Finishing Pigs," US Department of Agriculture, May 18, 2018, https://www.vetmed.umn.edu.

33 For information on PSS, see Tammy McCormick Donaldson, "Is Boredom Driving Pigs Crazy?," The University of Idaho College of Natural Resources, http://www.cnr.uidaho.edu, and Wayne Du, "Porcine Stress Syndrome Gene and Pork Production," Ontario Ministry of Agriculture Food and Rural Affairs, June 2004, https://trace.tennessee.edu. For information on the genetic basis of PTSD, see Aimee Midei, "Identification of the First Gene in Posttraumatic Stress Disorder," *Biomedicine.org*, September 22, 2002, http://news.bio-medicine.org .

34 Wayne Du, Ontario Ministry of Agriculture Food and Rural Affairs, June 2004, http://www.omafra.gov.on.ca.

35 Annette Charlotte Olsson, Jos Botermans, and Jan-Eric Englund, "Piglet Mortality—A Parallel Comparison Between Loose-Housed and Temporarily Confined Farrowing Sows in the Same Herd," *Acta Agriculturea Scandinavica* 68 (2018): 52–62, https://www.tandfonline.com.

36 E. Mainau, D. Temple, and X. Manteca, "Pre-Weaning Mortality in Piglets," Farm Animal Welfare Education Centre, January 2015, https://www.fawec.org.

37 PennState Extension, "Swine Production," June 20, 2005, https://extension.psu.edu.

38 PennState Extension, "Swine Production"; Andrew Jacobs, "Stealing Lauri: A Pig Kidnapping Highlights the Concerns over Antibiotics in Livestock," *New York Times*, August 4, 2019, https://www.nytimes.com.

39 National Agricultural Library, US Department of Agriculture, "Twenty-Eight Hour Law" (49 USC, Section 80502), March 17, 2020, 1219–20, www.nal.usda.gov.

40 Fiona Rioja-Lang, Jennifer A. Brown, Egan J. Brockhoff, and Luigi Faucitano, "A Review of Swine Transportation Research on Priority Welfare Issues: A Canadian Perspective," *Frontiers in Veterinary Science*, February 22, 2019, https://www.frontiersin.org.

41 Joe Vansickle, "Preparing Pigs for Transport," *National Hog Farmer*, September 15,. 2008, http://nationalhogfarmer.com.

42 Gail Eisnitz, *Slaughterhouse: The Shocking Story of Greed, Neglect, and Inhumane Treatment Inside the U.S. Meat Industry* (Amherst, NY: Prometheus Books, 1997), 102–104.

43 "My Visit to the Slaughterhouse: Crossing the Line Between Life and Meat," *Guardian*, August 29, 2014, https://www.theguardian.com.

44 Schlosser, "Fast Food Nation: Meat and Potatoes."

45 Eisnitz, *Slaughterhouse*, 68.

46 Food Safety and Inspection Service, Livestock Slaughter Inspection Training, "Human Handling of Livestock and Good Commercial Practices in Poultry," Livestock Slaughter Inspection Training, US Department of Agriculture, April 18, 2017, https://www.fsis.usda.gov.

47 Eisnitz, *Slaughterhouse*, 84.

48 Eisnitz, 93.

49 Wilson G. Pond, Fuller W. Bazer, Bernard E. Rollin (eds.), *Animal Welfare in Animal Agriculture* (Boca Raton: CRC Press, 2011), 151ff.

50 Peter J. Lammers, David R. Stender, and Mark S. Honeyman, "Mating or Inception," n.d., https://www.ipic.iastate.edu; Joe Vansickle, "Making 30

Pigs Per Sow Per Year Dream Come True," *National Hog Farmer*, January 15, 2009, https://www.nationalhogfarmer.com; Cheryl Day, "Increase in U.S. Sow Mortality a Real Mystery," *National Hog Farmer*, May 23, 2017, https://www.nationalhogfarmer.com; Iowa Pork Industry Center, "Iowa Pork Center Leads Industry-Wide Collaboration to Address Sow Mortality," Iowa State University, n.d., https://www.ipic.iastate.edu; Natalie James and Chris Cook, "Two Amputations a Week: The High Cost of Working in a US Meat Plant," Bureau of Investigative Journalism, May 7, 2018, https://www.thebureauinvestigates.com; Matthew Prescott, "Your Pig Almost Certainly Came from a Factory Farm, No Matter What Anyone Tells You," *Washington Post*, July 15, 2014, https://www.washingtonpost.com; Joshua Specht, "The Price of Plenty: How Beef Changed America," *Guardian*, May 7, 2019, https://www.theguardian.com; Animal Legal & Historical Center, Title 9—Animals and Animal Products; Chapter III—Food Safety and Inspection Service, Department of Agriculture; Subchapter A—Agency Organization and Terminology; Mandatory Meat and Poultry Products Inspection and Voluntary Inspection and Certification; Part 313—Humane Slaughter of Livestock; Natalie Jones, "Suffocation, Scalding, Heat Stress: Chickens Suffer 'Inexcusable' Welfare Breaches at US Abbatoirs," Bureau of Investigative Journalism, December 17, 2018, https://www.thebureauinvestigates.com; Madlen Davies and Andrew Wasley, "New Animal Cruelty Figures Show Need for Cameras," Bureau of Investigative Journalism, August 11, 2017, https://www.thebureauinvestigates.com; Occupational Safety and Health Administration, "Safety and Health Guide for the Meatpacking Industry," US Department of Labor, n.d., https://www.osha.gov; Matt McConnell, "'When We're Dead and Buried, Our Bones Will Keep Hurting': Workers Rights Under Threat in US Meat and Poultry Plants," Human Rights Watch, September 4, 2019, https://www.hrw.org; Mercy For Animals, "JBS Torture," n.d., http://jbstorture.com; Mercy For Animals, "Undercover Investigations," n.d. https://mercyforanimals.org.

51 Dylan Matthews, "America's Largest Pork Producer Pledged to Make Its Meat More Humane. An Investigation Says It Didn't," *Vox*, May 8, 2018, https://www.vox.com.

52 David Irvin, "Control Debate, Growers Advised," *Arkansas-Democrat Gazette*, Northwest Arkansas edition, September 22, 2007, https://scholar.google.com; Will Potter, "Whoever Defines the Issue Controls the Debate," Green Is the New Red, February 24, 2008, www.greenisthenewred.com.

53 Cited in Joan Dunayer, *Animal Equality: Language and Liberation* (Derwood, MD: Ryce Publishing, 2001), 138.

54 Dunayer, *Animal Equality*, 137.

55 Dunayer.

56 Cited in Fiddes, *Meat*, 96.

57 Michael Pollan, *The Omnivore's Dilemma: A Natural History of Four Meals* (New York: Penguin, 2006), 72.

58 Temple Grandin, "Evaluation of the Welfare of Cattle Housed in Outdoor Feedlot Pens," *Veterinary and Animal Science* 1–2 (2016): 23–28, https://www.sciencedirect.com.

59 Pollan, *The Omnivore's Dilemma*, 69.

60 See Clyde Lane, Jr. et al., "Castration of Beef Calves," *TheBeefSite.com: The Website for the Global Beef Industry*, January 2007, http://www.thebeefsite.com.

61 Michael Pollan, "Power Steer," *New York Times*, sec. 6, March 31, 2002; "Pollution from Giant Livestock Farms Threatens Public Health," National Resources Defense Council, July 15, 2005; Associated Press, "Nebraska Beef Recalls 1.2 Million Pounds of Meat," Fox News, January 13, 2105, https://www.foxnews.com.

62 Eilish Lynch, Mark McGee, and Bernadette Earley, "Weaning Management of Beef Calves with Implications for Animal Health and Welfare," *Journal of Applied Animal Research* 47 (2019): 167–75, https://doi.org/10.1080/0 9712119.2019.1594825; Daniel Enriquez, Maria J. Hötzel, and Rodolfo Ungerfeld, "Minimising the Stress of Weaning of Beef Calves: A Review," *Acta Veterinaria Scandinavica* 53, no. 1 (2011): 28, https://www.ncbi.nlm.nih.gov; Carolyn Stull, Sheila Barry, and Wayne Jensen, eds., *Beef Care Practices*, Publication 8257 (Davis: University of California, 2007).

63 Stan Smith, "Why Consider Backgrounding a Calf?," Ohio Beef Cattle Letter, The Ohio State University, August 28, 2019, https://u.osu.edu; US Department of Agriculture, "USDA Chief Scientist Statement on WHO Guidelines on Antibiotics," November 7, 2017, https://www.usda.gov/; Economic Research Service, "Sector at a Glance: U.S. Cattle Production and U.S. Beef and Cattle Trade," US Department of Agriculture, August 28, 2019, https://www.ers.usda.gov.

64 J. E. Lombard, C. B. Tucker, M. A. G. von Keyserlingk, C. A. Kopral, and D. M. Weary, "Associations Between Cow Hygiene, Hock Injuries, and Free Stall Usage on US Dairy Farms," *Journal of Dairy Science* 93 no. 10 (2010): 4668–76, https://www.sciencedirect.com; James Drouillard, "Current Situation and Future Trends for Beef Production in the United States of America—A Review," *Asian-Australasian Journal of Animal Sciences* 31, no. 7 (2018): 1007–16, Figure 2, https://www.ncbi.nlm.nih.gov; Temple Grandin, "Euthanasia and Slaughter of Livestock," *Journal American Veterinary Medical Association* 204 (1994): 1354–60, https://www.grandin.com; Chiara Disanto, Giuseppe Celano, Michele Varvara, Nunziana Fusiello, Armida Fransvea, Giancarlo Bozzo, and Gaetano Vitale Celano, "Stress Factors During Cattle Slaughter," *Italian Journal of Food Safety* 3, no. 3 (2014): 1682, https://www.ncbi.nlm.nih.gov.

65 Eisnitz, *Slaughterhouse*, 46.

66 Eisnitz, 43–44.

67 Schlosser, "Fast Food Nation: Meat and Potatoes."

68 Joby Warrick, "They Die Piece by Piece," *Washington Post*, April 10, 2001, https://www.uta.edu.

69 See Sandra Blakeslee, "Minds of Their Own: Birds Gain Respect," *New York Times*, February 1, 2005, http:// www.nytimes.com.

70 National Agriculture Statistics Service, *Poultry—Production and Value, 2018 Summary* (Washington, DC: USDA, 2019), https://www.nass.usda.gov.

71 University of Arkansas, "Poultry Feed Efficiency Research Has Implications for Human Health," January 4, 2018, https://news.uark.edu.

72 Poultry Service Association, *Poultry Handling and Transportation Manual* (Ontario, Canada: Poultry Service Association, 2017), http://www.poultryserviceassociation.com; Toby G. Knowles, Steve C. Kestin, Susan M. Haslam, Steven N. Brown, Laura E. Green, Andrew Butterworth, Stuart J. Pope, Dirk Pfeiffer, and Christine J. Nicol, "Leg Disorders in Broiler Chickens: Prevalence, Risk Factors and Prevention," *PLOS One* 3, no. 2 (2008): e1545, https://www.ncbi.nlm.nih.gov.

73 National Chicken Council, "Animal Welfare for Broiler Chickens," n.d., https://www.nationalchickencouncil.org.

74 Peter Singer, ed., *In Defense of Animals: The Second Wave* (Hoboken, NJ: Wiley-Blackwell, 2013).

75 Union of Concerned Scientists, "USDA Increases Line Speeds, Endangering Poultry Processing Plant Workers," January 9, 2019, https://www.ucsusa.org.

76 Josh Balk, "COK Investigation Exposes Chicken Industry Cruelty; Undercover Footage of Perdue Slaughter Plant Reveals Routine Abuse," Compassion Over Killing, https://animaloutlook.org.

77 Helen Harrison, "Why Infant Surgery without Anesthesia Went Unchallenged," *New York Times*, December 17, 1987 https://www.nytimes.com.

78 Lindsey Beaver, "Switzerland Bans Boiling Live Lobsters, but Scientists Wonder Why," *Washington Post*, reprinted in *New Zealand Herald*, January 14, 2018, https://www.nzherald.co.nz.

79 Rebecca Morelle, "Further Evidence Crabs and Other Crustaceans Feel Pain," BBC News, January 17, 2013, https://www.bbc.com.

80 For information on pain studies discussed in this section, see K. J. S. Anand, D. Phil, and P. R. Hickey, "Pain and Its Effects in the Human Neonate and Fetus," CIRP.org: The Circumcision Reference Library, September 5, 2006, http://www.cirp.org; K. J. S. Anand, D. Phil, and

P. R. Hickey. "Pain and its Effects in the Human Neonate and Fetus," *New England Journal of Medicine* 317, no. 21 (November 1987): 1321–29, http://www.cirp.org; Liz Austin, "Whole Foods Bans Sale of Live Lobsters," CBSnews.com, June 16, 2006, https://www.washingtontimes.com; David B. Chamberlain, "Babies Remember Pain," CIRP.org: The Circumcision Reference Library, December 15, 2006, http://www.cirp.org ; David B. Chamberlain. "Babies Remember Pain," *Journal of Prenatal and Perinatal Psychology and Health* 3, no. 4 (1989): 297–310, http://www.cirp.org; J. P. Chambers et al., "Self-Selection of the Analgesic Drug Carprofen by Lame Broiler Chickens," *Veterinary Record* 146, no. 11 (2000): 307–311. See also Mary T. Phillips, "Savages, Drunks, and Lab Animals: The Researcher's Perception of Pain," *Society and Animals* 1, no. 1 (1993): 61–81.

81 Jones, "Suffocation, Scalding, Heat Stress."

82 Joel L. Greene and Tadlock Cowan, *Table Egg Production and Hen Welfare: Agreement and Legislative Proposals* (Washington, DC: Congressional Research Service, 2014), https://fas.org.

83 Greene and Cowan, *Table Egg Production and Hen Welfare*; "How Hens Are Confined," *New York Times*, August 14, 2010, https://archive.nytimes.com.

84 Martin Hickman, "The End of Battery Farms in Britain—but Not Europe," *Independent*, December 27, 2011, https://www.independent.co.uk; Mattha Busby, "EU Imposes Hen Welfare Standards on Egg Imports for the First Time," *Guardian*, October 2, 2019, https://www.theguardian.com; Kelsey Piper, "Egg-Laying Hens Live in Horrific Conditions. Washington State Just Passed a Law to Change That," *Vox*, May 10, 2019, https://www.vox.com.

85 M. M. Bain, Y. Nys, and I. C. Dunn, "Increasing Persistency in Lay and Stabilising Egg Quality in Longer Laying Cycles. What Are the Challenges?," *British Poultry Science* 57, no. 3 (2016): 330–38, https://www.ncbi.nlm.nih.gov; M. N. Romanov and S. Weigend, "Breeding and Genetics: Analysis of Genetic Relationships between Various Populations of Domestic and Jungle Fowl Using Microsatellite Markers," *Poultry Science* 80, no. 8 (2001): 1057–63, https://doi.org.

86 Rodrigo A. Espinosa, "Prolapse of the Oviduct in Poultry," *MSD Manual Veterinary Manual*, n.d., https://www.msdvetmanual.com.

87 *Poultry Industry Manual: FAD PRep—Foreign Animal Disease Preparedness and Response Plan* (US Department of Agriculture, 2013), https://www.aphis.usda.gov; Compassion in World Farming, "The Life of: Laying Hens," Farm Animal Welfare Compendium, March 1, 2012, https://www.ciwf.org.uk.

88 Jia-rui Chong, "Wood-Chipped Chickens Fuel Outrage," *Los Angeles Times*, November 22, 2003, http://articles.latimes.com.

89 Lombard, et al., "Associations between Cow Hygiene, Hock Injuries, and Free Stall Usage"; Albert De Vries, Hailegziabher Dechassa, and Henk Hogeveen, "Economic Evaluation of Stall Stocking Density of Lactating Dairy Cows," *Journal of Dairy Science* 99, no. 5 (2016): 3848–57, https://www.sciencedirect.com.

90 American Cancer Society, "Recombinant Bovine Growth Hormone," n.d., https://www.cancer.org; US Department of Agriculture, *Dairy 2014: Health and Management Practices on U.S. Dairy Operations, 2014* (Fort Collins, CO: USDA, 2014), https://www.aphis.usda.gov.

91 US Department of Agriculture, *Dairy 2014*; Institute of Agriculture and Natural Resources, "Pregnant Cows, Timing of Pregnancy, Open Cows, Pregnancy Rate," University of Nebraska–Lincoln, n.d., https://beef.unl.edu.

92 John Dhuyvetter, "Winter Storm Information: Feeding Grain to Stock Cows," North Dakota State University, n.d., https://www.ag.ndsu.edu; Ron Scott, "Why Feed High-Fat Cattle Supplements," Purina Animal Nutrition, n.d., https://www.purinamills.com; US Food & Drug Administration, "Feed Ban Enhancement: Implementation Questions and Answers," n.d., https://www.fda.gov.

93 Food Safety and Inspection Service, "Veal from Farm to Table," US Department of Agriculture, August 6, 2013, https://www.fsis.usda.gov.

94 Julie Føske Johnsen et al., "The Effect of Nursing on the Cow–Calf Bond," *Applied Animal Behavior Science* (2014): 74, https://www.researchgate.net; Melissa C. Cantor, Heather W. Neave, and Joao H. C. Costa, "Current Perspectives on the Short- and Long-Term Effects of Conventional Dairy Calf Raising Systems: A Comparison with the Natural Environment," Translational Animal Science , no. 1 (2019): 549–63, https://doi.org; Kamil Hakan Dogan and Serafettin Demirci, "Livestock-Handling Related Injuries and Deaths," in *Livestock Production*, ed. Khalid Javed, IntechOpen, https://www.intechopen.com.

95 N. M. Nor, W. Steeneveld, and H. Hogeveen, "The Average Culling Rate of Dutch Dairy Herds over the Years 2007 to 2010 and Its Association with Herd Reproduction, Performance and Health," *Journal of Dairy Research* 81, no. 1 (2014): 1–8, https://www.ncbi.nlm.nih.gov.

96 Wyatt Bechtel, "Dairy Cattle Beef Up Beef Industry," *AgWeb*, November 6, 2014, https://www.agweb.com.

97 Humane Society Veterinary Medicine Association, "Facts on Veal Calves," 2018, https://www.hsvma.org.

98 Josh Stull, "USDA Proposes Changes to Improve Humane Handling of Veal Calves," Food Safety and Inspection Service, US Department of Agriculture, May 8, 2015, https://www.fsis.usda.gov.

99 CattleUSA.com, "Live Cattle Auctions," n.d., http://www.cattleusa. com; Empire Livestock Marketing, https://www.empirelivestock.com; Lanesboro Sales Commission, http://lanesborosalescommission.com.

100 CalfCare.ca, "Preventing Navel Infections in Newborn Calves," August 1, 2019, https://calfcare.ca.

101 American Veterinary Medical Association, "Welfare Implications of the Veal Calf Husbandry," October 13, 2008, www.avma.org; Food Safety and Inspection Service, US Department of Agriculture, "Veal from Farm to Table," March 5, 2020, www.fsis.usda.gov.

102 US Department of Agriculture, "Veal from Farm to Table."

103 Food Safety and Inspection Service, Livestock Slaughter Inspection Training, "Human Handling of Livestock and Good Commercial Practices in Poultry"; Food and Agriculture Organization of the United Nations, "Slaughter of Livestock," n.d., http://www.fao.org.

104 Eisnitz, *Slaughterhouse*, 43.

105 For information in this section on the cognitive abilities of sea animals, see the Humane Society of the United States website, available at https://www.humanesociety.org. Also see Culum Brown, Kevin Laland, and Jens Krause (eds.), *Fish Cognition and Behavior* (Oxford, UK: Blackwell Publishing, 2006), for an in-depth discussion of the cognitive abilities of fish; and Jeffrey Masson, *The Face on Your Plate: The Truth about Food* (New York: W.W. Norton, 2009).

106 Agence France-Presse, "World Briefing/Europe: Italy: City Wants Happier Goldfish," *New York Times*, July 24, 2004, https://www.nytimes.com.

107 For information in this section on the sentience of sea animals, see "Fish May Actually Feel Pain and React to It Much Like Humans Do," *Science Daily*, May 1, 2009, http://www.sciencedaily.com. This article gives a detailed description of the study on goldfish's response to increased temperatures. Also see Alex Kirby, "Fish Do Feel Pain, Scientists Say," BBC News Online, http://news.bbc.co.uk. This article discusses the first conclusive evidence of pain receptors in fish and describes the study where fish's lips were injected with an acidic substance. The original article on fish lip injection is from L. U. Sneddon, V. A. Braithwaite, and M. J. Gentle, "Do Fishes Have Nociceptors? Evidence for the Evolution of a Vertebrate Sensory System," *Proceedings of the Royal Society of London*, B 270. 1520 (June 7, 2003): 1115–21.

108 Harish, "How Many Animals Does a Vegetarian Save?"

109 For information on commercial and farm fishing, see Ken Jacobsen and Linda Riebel, *Eating to Save the Earth: Food Choices for a Healthy Planet* (Berkeley, CA: Celestial Arts, 2002). Also see Erik Marcus, *Meat Market: Animals, Ethics, and Money* (Ithaca, NY: Brio Press, 2005); https://www.

humanesociety.org; and Masson, *The Face on Your Plate*; Harish, "How Many Animals Does a Vegetarian Save?"

110 Food and Agriculture Organization of the United Nations, *The State of World Fisheries and Aquaculture: Meeting the Sustainable Development Goals* (Rome: FAO, 2018), http://www.fao.org; Mukhisa Kituyi and Peter Thomson, "90% of Fish Stocks Are Used Up—Fisheries Subsidies Must Stop," United Nations, July 13, 2018, https://unctad.org.

111 Food and Agriculture Organization of the United Nations, *The State of World Fisheries and Aquaculture*; Kituyi and Thomson, "90% of Fish Stocks Are Used Up"; Amy McDermott, "We Waste Almost Half of What We Catch: 5 Reasons That's Disastrous for the Oceans," Oceana, September 20, 2017, https://oceana.org.

112 Amanda Keledgian et al., *Wasted Catch: Unsolved Problems in U.S. Fisheries* (Washington, DC: Oceana, 2014), http://www.widecast.org; R. W. D. Davies, S. J. Cripps, A. Nickson, and G. Porter, "Defining and Estimating Global Marine Fisheries Bycatch," *Marine Policy* 33, no. 4 (2009): 661−72.

113 Ret Talbot, "'Holy Grail' Test for Illegal Cyanide-Caught Aquarium Fish May Be Fatally Flawed," *National Geographic*, June 25, 2018, https://www.nationalgeographic.com; Jani Actman, "Watch Fishermen Bomb Their Catch Out of the Water," *National Geographic*, June 3, 2016, https://www.nationalgeographic.com.

114 NOAA Fisheries, "Fisheries of the United States, 2017," n.d., https://www.fisheries.noaa.gov; Food and Agriculture Organization of the United Nations, *The State of World Fisheries and Aquaculture*.

115 Joel K. Bourne Jr., "How to Farm a Better Fish," *National Geographic*, June 2014, https://www.nationalgeographic.com; Celia A. Hoga, Fernanda L. Almeida, and Felix G. R. Reyes, "A Review on the Use of Hormones in Fish Farming: Analytical Methods to Determine Their Residues," *CyTA—Journal of Food* 16 (2018): 679−91, https://www.tandfonline.com; Samantha Horton, "Indiana Aquafarm Is Approved to Sell Genetically Modified Salmon," NPR, June 27, 2019, https://www.npr.org.

116 Center for Food Safety, "Ocean-Based Fish Farming: Pollution, Pathogens & Environmental Impacts," March 2015, https://www.centerforfood safety.org.

117 The Humane Society of the United States, "The Welfare of Animals in the Aquaculture Industry" (2008). *HSUS REPORTS. 5*, http://animal studiesrepository.org.

118 Dylan Matthews, "Cage-Free, Free Range, Organic: What All Those Egg Labels Really Mean," *Vox*, October 19, 2018, https://www.vox.com; Jennifer Chait, "Is Organic Livestock Production More Humane?," The Balance Small Business, June 26, 2019, https://www.thebalancesmb.com.

119 Damien McElroy, "Korean Outrage as West Tries to Use World Cup to Ban Dog Eating," *Telegraph*, January 6, 2002, http://www.telegraph.co.uk.

120 Schlosser, "Fast Food Nation: Meat and Potatoes."

121 Adam Andrzejewski, "Mapping the US Farm Subsidy $1M Club," *Forbes*, August 14, 2018, https://www.forbes.com.

122 Trevor J. Smith, *Corn, Cows, and Climate Change: How Federal Agricultural Subsidies Enable Factory Farming and Exacerbate U.S. Greenhouse Gas Emissions*, 9 *Washington Journal of Environmental Law & Policy* 26 (2019), https://digital commons.law.uw.edu.

123 Greenpeace, *Feeding the Problem: The Dangerous Intensification of Animal Farming in Europe* (Brussels, Belgium: Greenpeace, 2019), https://storage. googleapis.com.

124 For information on working conditions in the meatpacking industry, see Human Rights Watch, "Blood, Sweat and Fear," HRW.org, January 24, 2005, http://www.hrw.org; Lance Compa and Jamie Fellner, "Meatpacking's Human Toll," *Washington Post*, August 3, 2005, http:// www.washingtonpost.com; Megan Feldman, "Swift Meat Packing Plant and Illegal Immigrants," *Houston Press*, April 4, 2007, http:// www. houstonpress.com; Jeremy Rifkin, *Beyond Beef: The Rise and Fall of the Cattle Culture* (New York: Plume, 1992); Eric Schlosser, *Fast Food Nation: The Dark Side of the All-American Meal* (New York: Houghton Mifflin, 2001).

125 McConnell, "When We're Dead and Buried, Our Bones Will Keep Hurting."

126 For information on the effects of CAFOs on human health, see Mark Bittman, "Rethinking the Meat-Guzzler," *New York Times*, January 27, 2008, https://www.nytimes.com; Jennifer Lee, "Neighbors of Vast Hog Farms Say Foul Air Endangers Their Health," *New York Times*, May 11, 2003, http://www.nytimes.com; Pollan, "Power Steer"; National Resources Defense Council, "Pollution from Giant Livestock Farms Threatens Public Health," July 15, 2005, https://www.iatp.org; Johns Hopkins Bloomberg School of Public Health, "Public Health Association Calls for Moratorium on Factory Farms; Cites Health Issues, Pollution," January 9, 2004, http://www.jhsph.edu; McConnell, "'When We're Dead and Buried, Our Bones Will Keep Hurting.'"

127 McConnell, "'When We're Dead and Buried, Our Bones Will Keep Hurting.'"

128 Food Service and Inspection Service, US Department of Agriculture, "Modernization of Swine Slaughter Inspection," *Federal Register* 84, no. 190 (2019): 52300–49, https://www.fsis.usda.gov; OxFam America, *No Relief: Denial of Bathroom Breaks in the Poultry Industry* (Boston, MA: OxFam America, 2018), oxfamamerica.org.

129 Wendee Nicole, "CAFOs and Environmental Justice: The Case of North Carolina," *Environmental Health Perspectives* 121, no. 6 (2013): a182–a189, https://www.ncbi.nlm.nih.gov; Amy A. Schultz, Paul Peppard, Ron E. Gangnon, and Kristen M. C. Maleckia, "Residential Proximity to Concentrated Animal Feeding Operations and Allergic and Respiratory Disease," *Environment International* 130 (2019): 104911, https://www.science direct.com; JoAnn Burkholder, Bob Libra, Peter Weyer, Susan Heathcote, Dana Kolpin, Peter S. Thorne, and Michael Wichman, "Impacts of Waste from Concentrated Animal Feeding Operations on Water Quality," *Environmental Health Perspectives* 115, no. 2 (2007): 308–12, https://www.ncbi. nlm.nih.gov.

130 Renee Johnson, *The U.S.–EU Hormone Dispute* (Washington, DC: Congressional Research Service, 2015), https://fas.org.

131 See Michael Greger, *Bird Flu: A Virus of Our Own Hatching* (New York: Lantern Books, 2006); Rifkin, *Beyond Beef*; Union of Concerned Scientists, "They Eat What? The Reality of Feed at Animal Factories," *UCSUSA.org*, August 8, 2006, https://www.organicconsumers.org; and Johnson, *The U.S.–EU Hormone Dispute*.

132 Cited in Justin Ewers, "Don't Read This Over Dinner," *U.S. News and World Report* 139, no. 6 (August 7, 2005): 45.

133 WGBH Educational Foundation, "What Is HAACP," http://www.pbs. org, March 27, 2009 Also see Rifkin, *Beyond Beef*; Food Service and Inspection Service, US Department of Agriculture, "Modernization of Swine Slaughter Inspection."

134 Kimberly Kindy, "Pork Industry Soon Will Have More Power Over Meat Inspections," *Washington Post*, April 3, 2019, https://www.washington post.com; Food Service and Inspection Service, US Department of Agriculture, "Modernization of Swine Slaughter Inspection."

135 Kindy, "Pork Industry Soon Will Have More Power Over Meat Inspections"; McConnell, "'When We're Dead and Buried, Our Bones Will Keep Hurting.'"

136 Morgan Radford and Aaron Franco, "Inspectors Warn Unsafe Pork Could Make Its Way to Consumers Under Trump Rule Change," *NBC News*, December 16, 2019, https://www.nbcnews.com; Sentient Media, "The USDA Is Cutting Pig Slaughterhouse Rules: These Groups Are Fighting Back," December 23, 2019, https://sentientmedia.org.

137 National Antimicrobial Resistance Monitoring System, *2015 NARMS Integrated Report* (Washington, DC: US FDA, CDC, and USDA, 2015), https://www.fda.gov.

138 Gregor, *Bird Flu*; S. Pao, M. R. Ettinger, M. F. Khalid, A. O. Reid, and B. L. Nerrie, "Microbial Quality of Raw Aquacultured Fish Fillets Procured

from Internet and Local Retail Markets," *Journal of Food Protection* 71, no. 8 (August 2008): 1844–49; World Health Organization, *Review of Latest Available Evidence on Potential Transmission of Avian Influenza (H5N1) Through Water and Sewage and Ways to Reduce the Risks to Human Health* (Geneva, Switzerland, WHO, 2006) https://www.who.int; Physicians Committee for Responsible Medicine, "USDA Refuses to Protect Consumers from Fecal Contamination of Chicken and Other Meat," June 27, 2019, https://www.pcrm.org.

139 Greger, *Bird Flu*; World Health Organization, *Review of Latest Available Evidence on Potential Transmission of Avian Influenza*; Physicians Committee for Responsible Medicine, "USDA Refuses to Protect Consumers."

140 Consumer Federation of America, "Foodborne Illness Investigation Exposes Weakness in Meat and Poultry Inspection System," August 22, 2019, https://consumerfed.org.

141 Andrew Wasley, "'Dirty Meat': Shocking Hygiene Failings Discovered in US Pig and Chicken Plants," *Guardian*, February 21, 2018, https://www.theguardian.com.

142 Stephen J. Hedges and Washington Bureau, "E. Coli Loophole Cited in Recalls Tainted Meat Can Be Sold if Cooked," *Chicago Tribune*, November 11, 2007, http://archives.chicagotribune.com.

143 Bureau of Investigative Journalism, "Blowing the Whistle on the Meat Industry," September 19, 2017, https://www.thebureauinvestigates.com.

144 McConnell, "'When We're Dead and Buried, Our Bones Will Keep Hurting'"; Brett Bachman and Samantha Stokes, "Critics Worry About Food Safety as Federal Meat Inspectors Face Work Overload, Burnout," Midwest Center for Investigative Reporting, September 18, 2019, https://investigatemidwest.org.

145 Stephen J. Hedges and Washington Bureau, "Topps Meat Recall Raises Questions About Inspections Workload," *Chicago Tribune*, October 14, 2007, http://archives.chicagotribune.com.

146 US Bureau of Labor Statistics, "Labor Force Statistics from the Current Population Survey," January 22, 2020, https://www.bls.gov; Mary Jo Dudley, "These U.S. Industries Can't Work Without Illegal Immigrants," CBS News, January 10, 2019, https://www.cbsnews.com; Julia G. Young, "A Wall Can't Solve America's Addiction to Undocumented Immigration," *Washington Post*, January 9, 2019, https://www.washingtonpost.com; Food Service and Inspection Service, US Department of Agriculture, "Modernization of Swine Slaughter Inspection."

147 Schlosser, "Fast Food Nation: Meat and Potatoes."

148 Union of Concerned Scientists, "USDA Increases Line Speeds."

149 Eric Schlosser, "The Chain Never Stops," *Mother Jones*, July/August 2001, http://www.motherjones.com.

150 Amy Braunschweiger and Matt McConnell, "Interview: How the US Is Making Meatpacking Jobs Even More Dangerous," Human Rights Watch, September 4, 2019, https://www.hrw.org; James and Cook, "Two Amputations a Week"; Sean M. Smith, "How Safe Are the Workers Who Process Our Food?," *Monthly Labor Review*, US Bureau of Labor Statistics, July 2017, https://www.bls.gov; McConnell, "'When We're Dead and Buried, Our Bones Will Keep Hurting.'"

151 McConnell, "'When We're Dead and Buried, Our Bones Will Keep Hurting.'"

152 Schlosser, "The Chain Never Stops."

153 Human Rights Watch, "Blood, Sweat and Fear."

154 Eisnitz, *Slaughterhouse*, 87.

155 Eric B. Elbogen, Sally C. Johnson, H. Ryan Wagner, Connor Sullivan, Casey T. Taft, and Jean C. Beckham, "Violent Behaviour and Post-Traumatic Stress Disorder in US Iraq and Afghanistan Veterans," *British Journal of Psychiatry* 204, no. 5 (2014): 368–75, https://www.ncbi.nlm.nih.gov; Connor P. Sullivan and Eric B. Elbogen, "PTSD Symptoms and Family vs. Stranger Violence in Iraq and Afghanistan Veterans," *Law and Human Behavior* 38, no. 1 (2014): 1–9, https://www.ncbi.nlm.nih.gov.

156 Eisnitz, *Slaughterhouse*.

157 Eisnitz.

158 Eisnitz, 94.

159 Frederic J. Frommer, "Video Shows Workers Abusing Pigs," *Guardian Unlimited*, September 17, 2008, https://www.foxnews.com.

160 See Fiddes, *Meat*, and Simoons, *Eat Not This Flesh*.

161 Louis A. Berma, *Vegetarianism and the Jewish Tradition* (New York: Ktav Publishing, 1982), 13.

162 For information on the environmental effects of the meatpacking industry, see Jacobsen and Riebel, *Eating to Save the Earth*; Food and Agriculture Organization of the United Nations, "Livestock's Long Shadow: Environmental Issues and Options," 2006, http://www.fao.org; Daniel Ross, "Factory Farms Pollute the Environment and Poison Drinking Water," EcoWatch, February 20, 2019, https://www.ecowatch.com; Virginia Morell, "Meat-Eaters May Speed Worldwide Species Extinction, Study Warns," *Science*, August 11, 2015, https://www.sciencemag.org; Damian Carrington, "Avoiding Meat and Dairy Is 'Single Biggest Way' to Reduce Your Impact on Earth," *Guardian*, May 31, 2018, https://www.theguardian.com; Michael

Greger, "The Public Health Impacts of Concentrated Animal Feeding Operations on Local Communities," *Family and Community Health* 33, no. 1 (2010): 373–82, https://www.humanesociety.org.

163 Food and Agriculture Organization of the United Nations, "Livestock's Long Shadow"; Carrie Hribar, *Understanding Concentrated Animal Feeding Operations and Their Impact on Communities* (Bowling Green, OH: National Association of Local Boards of Health, 2010), https://www.cdc.gov; Nina Chestney and Stephanie Nebehay, "The UN Says We Need to Reduce Our Meat Consumption to Fight Climate Change and Improve Food Security," World Economic Forum, August 9, 2019, https://www.weforum.org; Francis Vergunst and Julian Savulescu, "Five Ways the Meat on Your Plate Is Killing the Planet," The Conversation, April 26, 2017, https://theconversation.com; Martin C. Heller, J. B. Ruhl, and Sacoby Wilson, "Court Ruling Is a First Step Toward Controlling Air Pollution from Livestock Farms," The Conversation, May 4, 2017, https://theconversation.com.

164 Johns Hopkins Bloomberg School of Public Health, "Public Health Association Calls for Moratorium on Factory Farms"; American Public Health Association, "Precautionary Moratorium on New Concentrated Animal Feed Operations," November 8, 2003, https://www.apha.org.

165 Center for Science in the Public Interest, http://www.cspinet.org/; Jacobsen and Riebel, *Eating to Save the Earth*; Food and Agriculture Organization of the United Nations, "Livestock's Long Shadow: Environmental Issues and Options"; Hribar, *Understanding Concentrated Animal Feeding Operations*; Chestney and Nebehay, "The UN Says We Need to Reduce Our Meat Consumption"; Vergunst and Savulescu, "Five Ways the Meat on Your Plate Is Killing the Planet"; D. Lee Miller and Gregory Muren, *CAFOs: What We Don't Know Is Hurting Us* (New York: Natural Resources Defense Council, 2019), https://www.nrdc.org; Heller, Ruhl, and Wilson, "Court Ruling Is a First Step."

166 Food and Agriculture Organization of the United Nations, "Livestock's Long Shadow."

167 William J. Ripple, Christopher Wolf, Thomas M. Newsome, Phoebe Barnard, and William R. Moomaw, "World Scientists' Warning of a Climate Emergency," *BioScience* 70, no. 1 (2020): 8–12, https://academic.oup.com; Damian Carrington, "Climate Crisis: 11,000 Scientists Warn of 'Untold Suffering,'" Guardian, November 5, 2019, https://www.theguardian.com; W. J. Ripple, C. Wolf, T. M. Newsome et al., :World Scientists' Warning of a Climate Emergency," *BioScience* 70, no. 1 (2020): 8–12, https://doi:10.1093/biosci/biz088.

168 Javier Mateo-Sagasta, Sara Marjani Zadeh, and Hugh Turral, *Water Pollution from Agriculture: A Global Review* (Rome: FAO, 2017), http://www.fao.org; Food and Agriculture Organization of the United Nations, "Livestock's Long Shadow."

169 B. Machovina, K. J. Feeley, and W. J. Ripple, "Biodiversity Conservation: The Key Is Reducing Meat Consumption," *Science of the Total Environment* 536 (2015): 419–31.

170 Food and Agriculture Organization of the United Nations, "Livestock's Long Shadow."

171 Claire Schnaffnit-Chatterjee, "The Global Food Equation: Food Security in an Environment of Increasing Scarcity," Deutsche Bank Research, September 21, 2009, https://www.dbresearch.com.

172 EPA, "Greenhouse Gas Emissions from a Typical Passenger Vehicle," March 2018, https://nepis.epa.gov; P. Gerber, H. Steinfeld, B. Henderson et al., *Tackling Climate Change Through Livestock: A Global Assessment of Emissions and Mitigation Opportunities* (Rome: FAO, 2013).

173 Select USA, "Agribusiness Spotlight: The Agribusiness Industry in the United States," n.d., https://www.selectusa.gov; James M. MacDonald, Robert A. Hoppe, and Doris Newton, *Three Decades of Consolidation in U.S. Agriculture*, EIB-189, US Department of Agriculture, Economic Research Service, March 2018, https://www.ers.usda.gov.

174 McConnell, "'When We're Dead and Buried, Our Bones Will Keep Hurting.'"

175 Philip Mattera, "USDA Inc.: How Agribusiness Has Hijacked Regulatory Policy at the U.S. Department of Agriculture," Corporate research project of Good Jobs First, July 23, 2004, https://www.competitivemarkets.com.

176 Mattera, "USDA Inc."

177 FarmFutures, "Craig Morris Leaving USDA to Join National Pork Board," October 18, 2017, https://www.farmprogress.com.

178 JBS USA, "JBS Names Former U.S. Department of Agriculture Deputy Under Secretary for Food Safety as Global Head of Food Safety and Quality Assurance," August 3, 2017, https://jbssa.com.

179 OpenSecrets.org, "Livestock: Money to Congress," 2018, https://www.opensecrets.org.

180 National Sustainable Agriculture Coalition, "Cover Crops and CAFOs: An Analysis of 2016 EQIP Spending," January 12, 2017, https://sustainableagriculture.net; Union of Concerned Scientists, "EPA Stops Collecting Data on Pollutants Released from Farms," August 5, 2019, https://www.ucsusa.org.

181 Simply Wall St., "CEO Compensation Analysis: Conagra Brands," accessed March 3, 2020, https://simplywall.st.

182 See Centers for Disease Control, "Multistate Outbreak of *Escherichia coli* O157:H7 Infections Associated with Eating Ground Beef—United

States, June–July 2002," July 26, 2002, http://www.cdc.gov; see also "About E. Coli," http://www.about-ecoli.com.

183 W. C. Willett, "Balancing Lifestyle and Genomics Research for Disease Prevention," *Science* 296 (2002):695–98; Walter C. Willett, Jeffrey P. Koplan, Rachel Nugent, Courtenay Dusenbury, Pekka Puska, and Thomas A. Gaziano, *Disease Control Priorities in Developing Countries* 2nd ed. (Washington, DC: The International Bank for Reconstruction and Development/The World Bank; New York: Oxford University Press, 2006), Chapter 44, https://www.ncbi.nlm.nih.gov.

184 C. G. Corey et al., "US Adult Cigar Smoking Patterns, Purchasing Behaviors, and Reasons for Use According to Cigar Type: Findings from the Population Assessment of Tobacco and Health (PATH) Study, 2013–2014," *Nicotine & Tobacco Research* 20, no. 12 (2018): 1457–66, https://www.ncbi.nlm.nih.gov.

185 Heinrich Böll Stiftung, *Meat Atlas: Facts and Figures About the Animals We Eat* (Berlin, Germany: Heinrich Böll Foundation; Brussels, Belgium: Friends of the Earth, Europe, 2014), 56, http://www.foeeurope.org; Niall McCarthy, "Who Are America's Vegans and Vegetarians," *Forbes*, August 6, 2018, https://www.forbes.com.

186 Rob M. van Dam et al., "Dietary Fat and Meat Intake in Relation to Risk of Type 2 Diabetes in Men." *Diabetes Care* 25, no. 3 (March 1, 2002): 417–24, https://doi.org; An Pan et al., "Changes in Red Meat Consumption and Subsequent Risk of Type 2 Diabetes Mellitus: Three Cohorts of US Men and Women," *JAMA Internal Medicine* 173, no. 14 (July 22, 2013): 1328–35, https://doi.org; Geertruida J. van Woudenbergh et al., "Eating Fish and Risk of Type 2 Diabetes," *Diabetes Care* 32, no. 11 (November 2009): 2021–26, https://doi.org.

187 Genevieve Tse and Guy D. Eslick, "Egg Consumption and Risk of GI Neoplasms: Dose-Response Meta-Analysis and Systematic Review," *European Journal of Nutrition* 53, no. 7 (October 2014): 1581–90, https://doi.org; Elizabeth A. Platz, Steven K. Clinton, and Edward Giovannucci, "Association Between Plasma Cholesterol and Prostate Cancer in the PSA Era," *International Journal of Cancer* 123, no. 7 (October 1, 2008): 1693–98, https://doi.org; Kristine Pelton, Michael R. Freeman, and Keith R. Solomon, "Cholesterol and Prostate Cancer," *Current Opinion in Pharmacology* 12, no. 6 (December 2012): 751–59, https://doi.org.

188 N. Bergeron, S. Chiu, P. T. Williams, S., King, and R. M. Krauss, "Effects of Red Meat, White Meat, and Nonmeat Protein Sources on Atherogenic Lipoprotein Measures in the Context of Low Compared with High Saturated Fat Intake: A Randomized Controlled Trial," *American Journal of Clinical Nutrition* 110, no. 1 (2019): 24–33, https://doi.org.

189 M. Yang, S. A. Kenfield, E. L. Van Blarigan, K. M. Wilson, J. L. Batista, H. D. Sesso et al., "Dairy Intake After Prostate Cancer Diagnosis in

Relation to Disease-Specific and Total Mortality," *International Journal of Cancer* 137, no. 10 (2015): 2462–69, https://doi.org.

190 Center for Food Safety, *America's Secret Animal Drug Problem: How Lack of Transparency Is Endangering Human Health and Animal Welfare* (Washington, DC: Center for Food Safety, 2015), http://www.centerforfoodsafety.org; Michael Pollan, "Power Steer," *New York Times*, March 31, 2002, https://www.nytimes.com; US Food and Drug Administration, "Feed Ban Enhancement: Implementation Questions and Answers," n.d., https://www.fda.gov; C. R. Hamilton, "Real and Perceived Issues Involving Animal Proteins," n.d., http://www.fao.org.

191 EDSitement, "Voting Rights for Women: Pro and Anti-Suffrage," June 19, 2019, https://edsitement.neh.gov.

192 American Veterinary Medical Association, "Welfare Implications of Gestation Sow Housing," November 19, 2015, https://www.avma.org.

193 Robert Jay Lifton and Eric Markusen, *The Genocidal Mentality: Nazi Holocaust and Nuclear Threat* (New York: Basic Books, 1990). The authors use these terms to describe professionals who support nuclear development.

194 Lifton and Markusen, *The Genocidal Mentality*.

195 Dietitians for Professional Integrity, "Concerns About Dairy Industry Sponsorship," September 26, 2015, https://integritydietitians.org; International Dairy Foods Association, "Government's 2015 Dietary Guidelines Affirms Role of Dairy Foods in Healthy Eating Patterns," January 7, 2016, https://www.idfa.org.

196 Information on the ADA's Corporate Sponsorship Program is available at http://www.eatrightpro.org.

197 NutritionFacts.org, "Dairy & Cancer," March 13, 2019, https://nutrition facts.org; Ingegerd Johansson, Lena Maria Nilsson, Anders Esberg, Jan-Håkan Jansson, and Anna Winkvist, "Dairy Intake Revisited— Associations between Dairy Intake and Lifestyle Related Cardio-Metabolic Risk Factors in a High Milk Consuming Population," *Nutrition Journal* 17, no. 110 (2018), https://doi.org; W. Lu et al., "Dairy Products Intake and Cancer Mortality Risk: A Meta-Analysis of 11 Population-Based Cohort Studies," *Nutrition Journal* 15, no. 91 (2016), https://doi.org.

198 K. I. Mills, "More Shocking Results: New Research Replicates Milgram's Findings," Monitor on Psychology 40, no. 3 (2009): 13, https://www.apa.org.

199 See Allan G. Johnson, *Privilege, Power, and Difference* (New York: McGraw-Hill Education, 2005).

200 Robert Jay Lifton, *The Nazi Doctors: Medical Killing and the Psychology of Genocide* (New York: Basic Books, 1986); Lifton and Markusen, *The Genocidal Mentality*.

201 For more information on the meat-masculinity connection, see Fiddes, *Meat*. Also see Carol J. Adams and Josephine Donovan, *Animals and Women: Feminist Theoretical Explorations* (Durham, NC: Duke University Press, 1995); and Carol J. Adams, *The Sexual Politics of Meat: A Feminist-Vegetarian Critical Theory* (New York: Continuum, 1992).

202 Physicians Committee for Responsible Medicine, "The Protein Myth," http://www.pcrm.org.

203 Lifton, *The Nazi Doctors*; Lifton and Markusen, *The Genocidal Mentality*.

204 Farb and Armelagos, *Consuming Passions*.

205 Paul Slovic, "If I Look at the Mass I Will Never Act: Psychic Numbing and Genocide," *Judgment and Decision Making* 2, no. 2 (2007): 79–95.

206 For information on morality and disgust, see works cited in the bibliography by Rozin et al. Also see Andras Angyal, "Disgust and Related Aversions," *Journal of Abnormal and Social Psychology* 36 (1941): 393–412; Michael Lemonick, "Why We Get Disgusted," *Time*, May 24, 2007, http://www.time.com; Simone Schnall, Jonathan Haidt, and Gerald L. Clore, "Disgust as Embodied Moral Judgment," *Personality and Social Psychology Bulletin* 34, no. 8 (2008): 1096–1109; Trine Tsouderos, "Some Facial Expressions Are Part of a Primal 'Disgust Response,' University of Toronto Study Finds," *Chicago Tribune*, February 27, 2009, https://www. thehour.com; and Thalia Wheatley and Jonathon Haidt, "Hypnotically Induced Disgust Makes Moral Judgments More Severe," *Psychological Science* 16 (2005): 780–84.

207 Tsouderos, "Some Facial Expressions."

208 Simoons, *Eat Not This Flesh*, 106.

209 Farb and Armelagos, *Consuming Passions*, 167.

210 Kathy Berghorn, "Emily the Sacred Cow: Lewis Has Asked Me to Put Down Some of My Thoughts on Emily," April 2, 2003, http://www. peaceabbey.org.

211 Judith Herman, *Trauma and Recovery: The Aftermath of Violence—From Domestic Abuse to Political Terror* (New York: Basic Books, 1997), 1.

212 Sandra Blakeslee, "Cells that Read Minds," *New York Times*, January 10, 2006, https://www.nytimes.com; V. S. Ramachandran, "Mirror Neurons and the Brain in the Vat," *Edge: The Third Culture*, January 10, 2006, http://www.edge.org; and "Children Are Naturally Prone to Be Empathic and Moral," *Science Daily*, July 12, 2008, http://www.science daily.com.

213 From *The Witness* directed by Jenny Stein and produced by James LaVeck (Tribe of Heart Production Company, 2000).

214 Cited in Charles Patterson, *Eternal Treblinka: Our Treatment of Animals and the Holocaust* (New York: Lantern Books, 2002), 231.

215 Matthew Scully, *Dominion: The Power of Man, the Suffering of Animals, and the Call to Mercy* (New York: St. Martin's Press, 2002), 394.

216 All information in this paragraph is from the Union of Concerned Scientists, September 1, 2008, http://www.ucsusa.org. See also notes from chapter 4; Intergovernmental Panel on Climate Change, *Climate Change and Land* (Geneva, Switzerland: IPCC, 2019), https://www.ipcc.ch; Food and Agriculture Organization of the United Nations, "Livestock and Environment," November 22, 2013, http://www.fao.org.

217 Grand View Research, "Vegan Food Market Size, Share & Trends Analysis Report by Product (Dairy Alternative, Meat Substitute), by Distribution Channel (Online Offline), by Region (APAC, CSA, MEA, Europe, North America), and Segment Forecasts, 2019–2025," June 2019, https://www.grandviewresearch.com.

218 James O'Dea, "Witnessing: A Form of Compassion," March 2, 2007, http://awakin.org.

219 Cited in Patterson, *Eternal Treblinka*, 137.

220 Herman, *Trauma and Recovery*, 247.

Resources

Following is a small selection of materials to help you take the next steps in moving beyond carnism.

Beyond Beliefs: A Guide to Improving Relationships and Communication for Vegans, Vegetarians, and Meat Eaters, by Melanie Joy (Lantern Books, 2018)
> an overview of the principles and tools for healthy relating, applied to relationships where at least one person is vegan (or vegetarian)

Animal Liberation, by Peter Singer (Harper Perennial Modern Classics, Reissue edition 2009)
> a philosophical examination of the basis of carnism

Eating Animals, by Jonathan Safran Foer (Back Bay Books, 2010)
> a compelling examination of the foundations and practices of carnistic consumption

How Not to Die: Discover the Foods Scientifically Proven to Prevent and Reverse Disease, by Michael Greger (Flatiron Books, 2015)
> an encyclopedic guide to preventing and reversing disease and to living healthfully

nutritionfacts.org
> Dr. Greger's comprehensive, video-based website about nutrition

Beyond Carnism (*carnism.org*)
> my organization, with videos and other resources to help raise awareness of and transform carnism

Challenge 22 (*challenge22.com*)
> an online 22-day vegan challenge, which includes guidance and support for those wishing to try veganism

Veganuary (veganuary.com)
> an organization offering a vegan challenge, starter kit, and other tips and resources to help people move toward veganism

Bosh (*bosh.tv*)
> an engaging, informative, and comprehensive selection of cooking videos with select resources

Happy Cow (*happycow.net*)
> a website and app to locate vegan and vegan-friendly stores and restaurants around the world

Selected Bibliography

Adams, Carol J. "Feeding on Grace: Institutional Violence, Christianity, and Vegetarianism." In *Good News for Animals? Christian Approaches to Animal Well-Being*, edited by C. Pinches and J. B. McDaniel, 143–59. Maryknoll, NY: Orbis, 1993.

———. *Living Among Meat Eaters: The Vegetarian's Survival Handbook*. New York: Three Rivers Press, 2001.

———. *Neither Man nor Beast: Feminism and the Defense of Animals*. New York: Continuum, 1995.

———. *The Sexual Politics of Meat: A Feminist-Vegetarian Critical Theory*. New York: Continuum, 1992.

Adams, Carol J., and Josephine Donovan, eds. *Animals and Women: Feminist Theoretical Explorations*. Durham, NC: Duke University Press, 1995.

Allen, Michael, et al. "Values and Beliefs of Vegetarians and Omnivores." *Journal of Social Psychology* 140, no. 4 (2000): 405–22.

Allport, Gordon. *The Nature of Prejudice*. New York: Addison-Wesley, 1958.

American Veterinary Medical Association. "Welfare Implications of the Veal Calf Husbandry." October 13, 2008. Accessed March 27, 2009. http://www.avma.org.

Anand, K. J. S., D. Phil, and P. R. Hickey. "Pain and Its Effects in the Human Neonate and Fetus." *New England Journal of Medicine* 317, no. 21. (1987): 1321–29. Accessed March 4, 2020. http://www.cirp.org.

———. CIRP.org: The Circumcision Reference Library. September 5, 2006. Accessed March 4, 2020. http://www.cirp.org.

Angyal, Andras. "Disgust and Related Aversions." *Journal of Abnormal and Social Psychology* 36 (1941): 393–412.

"Animal Cruelty Laws Among Fastest-Growing." MSNBC. February 15, 2009. Accessed March 26, 2009. http://www.msnbc.msn.com.

Araki, H., et al. "High-Risk Group for Benign Prostatic Hypertrophy." *Prostate* 4, no. 3 (1983): 253–64. Accessed March 4, 2020. http://www.ncbi.nlm.nih.gov.

Arluke, Arnold. "Uneasiness Among Laboratory Technicians." *Lab Animal* 19, no. 4 (1990): 20–39.

Arluke, Arnold, and Frederic Hafferty. "From Apprehension to Fascination with 'Dog Lab': The Use of Absolutions by Medical Students." *Journal of Contemporary Ethnography* 25, no. 2 (1996): 201–25.

Arluke, Arnold, and Clinton Sanders. *Regarding Animals.* Philadelphia: Temple University Press, 1996.

Aronson, Elliot. "Back to the Future: Retrospective Review of Leon Festinger's A Theory of Cognitive Dissonance." *American Journal of Psychology* 110 (1997): 127–37.

———. "Dissonance, Hypocrisy, and the Self-Concept." In *Cognitive Dissonance: Progress on a Pivotal Theory in Social Psychology,* edited by E. Harmon-Jones and J. Mills, 103–26. Washington, DC: American Psychological Association, 1999.

Ascherio, Alberto, Graham A. Colditz, Edward Giovannucci, Eric B. Rimm, Meir J. Stampfer, and Walter C. Willett. "Intake of Fat, Meat, and Fiber in Relation to Risk of Colon Cancer in Men." *Cancer Research* 54 (1994): 2390–97.

Augoustinos, Martha, and Katherine Reynolds, eds. *Understanding Prejudice, Racism, and Social Conflict.* Thousand Oaks, CA: Sage Publications, 2001.

Austin, Liz. "Whole Foods Bans Sale of Live Lobsters." CBS News. June 16, 2006. Accessed March 27, 2009. http://www.cbsnews.com.

Barrows, Anita. "The Ecopsychology of Child Development." In *Ecopsychology: Restoring the Earth, Healing the Mind,* edited by T. Roszak, M. E. Gomes, and D. Kanner, 101–110. San Francisco: Sierra Club Books, 1995.

Barthes, Roland. "Toward a Psychosociology of Contemporary Food Consumption." In *Food and Drink in History: Selections from the Annales Economies, Societies, Civilisations: Vol. 5,* edited by Robert Forster and Orest Ranum, 166–73. Baltimore and London: Johns Hopkins University Press, 1979.

Beardsworth, Alan, and Teresa Keil. "Contemporary Vegetarianism in the U.K.: Challenge and Incorporation?" *Appetite* 20 (1993): 229–34.

———. "The Vegetarian Option: Varieties, Conversions, Motives and Careers." *The Sociological Review* 40 (1992): 253–93.

Belasco, Warren. "Food, Morality, and Social Reform." In *Morality and Health,* edited by Allen Brandt and Paul Rozin, 185–99. New York: Rutledge, 1997.

Bell, A. Chris, et al. "A Method for Describing Food Beliefs which May Predict Personal Food Choice." *Journal of Nutrition Education* 13, no. 1 (1981): 22–26.

Bhatnagar, Parija. "PETA's Impotence Ad a No-No with CBS." CNN. January 15, 2004. Accessed March 4, 2020. http://money.cnn.com.

Biermann-Ratjen, Eva Maria. "Incongruence and Psychopathology." In *Person-Centered Therapy: A European Perspective,* edited by B. Thorne and E. Lambers, 119–30. London: Sage Publications, 1998.

Bittman, Julie Cart. "Land Study on Grazing Denounced," *Los Angeles Times,* June 18, 2005. Accessed March 4, 2020. http://articles.latimes.com.

Bittman, Mark. "Cells that Read Minds." *New York Times.* January 10, 2006. Accessed March 4, 2020. http://www.nytimes.com.

———. "Rethinking the Meat-Guzzler." *New York Times.* January 27, 2008. Accessed March 4, 2020. http://www.nytimes.com.

Blakeslee, Sandra. "Minds of Their Own: Birds Gain Respect." *New York Times.* February 1, 2005. Accessed March 4, 2020. http://www.nytimes.com.

Boat, Barbara. "The Relationship between Violence to Children and Violence to Animals: An Ignored Link?" *Journal of Interpersonal Violence* 10, no. 2 (1995): 228–35.

Booth, David. *The Psychology of Nutrition.* Bristol, PA: Taylor & Francis, 1994.

Brown, Culum, Kevin Laland, and Jens Krause, eds. *Fish Cognition and Behavior.* Oxford, UK: Blackwell Publishing, 2006.

Brown, Lesley Melville. *Cruelty to Animals: The Moral Debt.* London: Macmillan Press, 1988.

Calkins, A. "Observations on Vegetarian Dietary Practice and Social Factors: The Need for Further Research." *Perspectives in Practice* 74 (1979): 353–55.

Campbell, T. Colin, and Thomas M. Campell. *The China Study: The Most Comprehensive Study of Nutrition Ever Conducted and the Startling Implications for Diet, Weight Loss and Long-Term Health.* Dallas: Benbella Books, 2006.

Cart, Julie. "Land Study on Grazing Denounced." *Los Angeles Times* June 18, 2005. Accessed March 4, 2020. http://articles.latimes.com.

Center for Responsive Politics. "Money in Politics—See Who's Giving and Who's Getting." Accessed March 4, 2020. http://www.opensecrets.org.

Center for Science in the Public Interest (CSPI). Accessed March 4, 2020. http://www.cspinet.org.

Chamberlain, David B. "Babies Remember Pain." *CIRP.org:* The Circumcision Reference Library. December 15, 2006. Accessed March 4, 2020. http://www.cirp.org.

———."Babies Remember Pain." *Journal of Prenatal and Perinatal Psychology and Health* 3, no. 4 (1989): 297–310. Accessed March 4, 2020. http://www.cirp.org.

Chambers, J. P., et al. "Self-Selection of the Analgesic Drug Carprofen by Lame Broiler Chickens." *The Veterinary Record* 146, no. 11 (2000): 307–11.

Chambers, P. G., et al. "Slaughter of Livestock." Food and Agriculture Organization of the United Nations. April 2001. Accessed March 4, 2020. http://www.fao.org.

"Children Are Naturally Prone to Be Empathic and Moral." *Science Daily.* July 12, 2008. Accessed March 4, 2020. http://www.sciencedaily.com.

Chong, Jia-rui. "Wood-Chipped Chickens Fuel Outrage." *Los Angeles Times.* November 22, 2003. Accessed March 4, 2020. http://articles.latimes.com.

Clarke, Paul, and Andrew Linzey. *Political Theory and Animal Rights.* Winchester, MA: Pluto Press, 1990.

Colditz, G. A., et al. "Relation of Meat, Fat, and Fiber Intake to the Risk of Colon Cancer in a Prospective Study Among Women." *New England Journal of Medicine* 323, no. 24 (1990): 1664–72.

Compa, Lance, and Jamie Fellner. "Meatpacking's Human Toll." *Washington Post.* August 3, 2005. Accessed March 4, 2020. http://www.washingtonpost.com.

Comstock, Gary L. "Pigs and Piety: A Theocentric Perspective on Food Animals." In *Good News for Animals? Christian Approaches to Animal Well-Being*, edited by Charles Pinches and Jay B. McDaniel, 105–27. Maryknoll, NY: Orbis, 1993.

Cone, Tracie. "Dairy Cows Head for Slaughter as Milk Prices Sour." Associated Press. February 16, 2009. Accessed March 4, 2020. http://www3.signonsandiego.com.

Conrad, Peter, and Joseph Schneider. *Deviance and Medicalization: From Badness to Sickness.* Toronto: C.V. Mosby & Co., 1980.

Cooper, Charles, Thomas Wise, and Lee Mann. "Psychological and Cognitive Characteristics of Vegetarians." *Psychosomatics* 26, no. 6 (1985): 521–27.

Counihan, Carol M. "Food Rules in the United States: Individualism, Control, and Hierarchy." *Anthropological Quarterly* 65 (1992): 55–66.

Davis, Karen. "Thinking Like a Chicken: Farm Animals and the Feminine Connection." In *Animals and Women: Feminist Theoretical Explorations*, edited by Carol J. Adams and Josephine Donovan, 192–212. Durham, NC: Duke University Press, 1995.

Dawn, Karen. *Thanking the Monkey: Rethinking the Way We Treat Animals.* New York: Harper, 2008.

Descartes, Rene. *A Discourse on the Method (Oxford World's Classics).* Translated by Ian Maclean. New York: Oxford University Press, 2006.

Devine, Tom. "Shielding the Giant: USDA's 'Don't Look, Don't Know' Policy for Beef Inspection." *WhistleBlower.org.* Accessed March 27, 2009. http://www.whistleblower.org.

Dietz, Thomas, et al. "Social Psychological and Structural Influences on Vegetarian Beliefs." *Rural Sociology* 64, no. 3 (1999): 500–11.

———, et al. "Values and Vegetarianism: An Exploratory Analysis." *Rural Sociology* 60, no. 3 (1995): 533–42.

Dilanian, Ken. "Bill Includes Billions in Farm Subsidies." *USA Today.* May 15, 2008. Accessed March 25, 2009. http://www.usatoday.com.

Donaldson, Tammy McCormick. "Is Boredom Driving Pigs Crazy?" Working paper, the University of Idaho College of Natural Resources. Accessed March 26, 2009. http://www.cnr.uidaho.edu.

Douglas, Mary. *Implicit Meanings: Essays in Anthropology.* London: Routledge & Kegan Paul, 1975.

Draycott, Simon, and Alan Dabbs. "Cognitive Dissonance: An Overview of the Literature and its Integration into Theory and Practice in Clinical Psychology." *British Journal of Clinical Psychology* 37 (1998): 341–53.

Du, Wayne. "Porcine Stress Syndrome Gene and Pork Production." Ontario Ministry of Agriculture Food and Rural Affairs. June 2004. Accessed March 27, 2009. http://www.omafra.gov.on.ca.

Dunayer, Joan. *Animal Equality: Language and Liberation.* Derwood, MD: Ryce Publishing, 2001.

Eisler, Riane. *The Chalice and the Blade: Our History, Our Future.* New York: HarperCollins, 1987.

Eisnitz, Gail. *Slaughterhouse: The Shocking Story of Greed, Neglect, and Inhumane Treatment Inside the U.S. Meat Industry.* Amherst, NY: Prometheus Books, 1997.

Esselstyn, Caldwell B. *Prevent and Reverse Heart Disease: The Revolutionary, Scientifically Proven, Nutrition-Based Cure.* New York: Penguin, 2008.

Ewers, Justin. "Don't Read This Over Dinner." *U.S. News and World Report.* August 7, 2005. Accessed March 31, 2009. http://www.usnews.com.

"EWG Farm Bill 2007 Policy Analysis Database." *Environmental Working Group.* Accessed March 25, 2009. http://farm.ewg.org.

Farb, Peter, and George Armelagos. *Consuming Passions: The Anthropology of Eating.* Boston: Houghton Mifflin, 1980.

Feldman, Megan. "Swift Meat Packing Plant and Illegal Immigrants." *The Houston Press.* April 4, 2007. Accessed March 4, 2020. http://www.houston press.com.

Fessler, Daniel M. T., and Carlos David Navarrete. "Meat Is Good to Taboo: Dietary Proscriptions as a Product of the Interaction of Psychological Mechanisms and Social Processes." *Journal of Cognition and Culture* 3, no. 1 (2003): 1–40. Accessed March 4, 2020. http://www.sscnet.ucla.edu.

———. UCLA. Accessed March 4, 2020. http://www.sscnet.ucla.edu/ anthro/faculty/fessler/pubs/MeatIsGoodToTaboo.pdf.

Festinger, Leon. *A Theory of Cognitive Dissonance.* Evanston, IL: Row, Peterson, 1957.

Fiddes, Nick. *Meat: A Natural Symbol.* New York: Rutledge, 1991.

Finsen, Lawrence, and Susan Finsen. *The Animal Rights Movement in America: From Compassion to Respect.* New York: Twayne Publishers, 1994.

Fischler, Claude. "Food Habits, Social Change and the Nature/Culture Dilemma." *Social Science Information* 19, no. 6 (1980): 937–53.

———. "Food, Self and Identity." *Social Science Information.* 27, no. 2 (1988): 275–92.

"Fish May Actually Feel Pain and React to It Much Like Humans Do." *Science Daily.* May 1, 2009. Accessed March 4, 2020. http://www.sciencedaily.com.

Food and Agriculture Organization of the United Nations. "Livestock's Long Shadow: Environmental Issues and Options." 2006. Accessed March 4, 2020. http://www.fao.org.

———. "Pro-Poor Livestock Policy Initiative." Accessed March 26, 2009. http://www.fao.org.

"Food Taboos: It's All a Matter of Taste." *National Geographic News.* April 19, 2004. Accessed March 26, 2009. http://news.nationalgeographic.com.

Fox, Michael Allen. *Deep Vegetarianism.* Philadelphia: Temple University Press, 1999.

Francione, Gary. *Animals, Property, and the Law.* Philadelphia: Temple University Press, 1995.

Friedman, Stanley. "On Vegetarianism." *Journal of the American Psychoanalytic Association* 23, no. 2 (1975): 396–406.

Frommer, Frederic J. "Video Shows Workers Abusing Pigs." *The Guardian Unlimited.* September 17, 2008. Accessed March 31, 2009. http://www.guardian.co.uk.

Furst, Tanis, et al. "Food Choice: A Conceptual Model of the Process." *Appetite* 26 (1996): 247–66.

Garner, Robert, ed. *Animal Rights: The Changing Debate.* New York: New York University Press, 1996.

Gaudette, Karen. "USDA Expands Ground-Beef Recall." *Seattle Times.* July 4, 2008. Accessed March 27, 2009. http://seattletimes.nwsource.com.

Gofton, L. "The Rules of the Table: Sociological Factors Influencing Food Choice." In *The Food Consumer,* by Christopher Ritson, Leslie Gofton, and John McKenzie, 127–53. New York: John Wiley & Sons, 1986.

Greger, Michael. *Bird Flu: A Virus of Our Own Hatching.* New York: Lantern Books, 2006.

Grossman, Dave. *On Killing: The Psychological Cost of Learning to Kill in War and Society.* New York: Back Bay Books, 1996.

Gurian-Sherman, Doug. "CAFOs Uncovered: The Untold Costs of Confined Animal Feeding Operations." Union of Concerned Scientists. April 2008. Accessed March 31, 2009. http://www.ucsusa.org.

Halpin, Zuleyma Tang. "Scientific Objectivity and the Concept of the 'Other.'" *Women's Studies International Forum* 12, no. 3 (1989): 285–94.

Hamilton, Malcolm. "Wholefoods and Healthfoods: Beliefs and Attitudes." *Appetite* 20 (1993): 223–28.

Harmon-Jones, Eddie, and Judson Mills, eds. *Cognitive Dissonance: Progress on a Pivotal Theory in Social Psychology.* Washington, DC: American Psychological Association, 1999.

Hedges, Stephen J., and Washington Bureau. "E. Coli Loophole Cited in Recalls Tainted Meat Can Be Sold if Cooked." *Chicago Tribune.* November 11, 2007. Accessed March 27, 2009. http://archives.chicagotribune.com.

———. "Topps Meat Recall Raises Questions About Inspections Workload." *Chicago Tribune.* October 14, 2007. Accessed March 27, 2009. http:// archives.chicagotribune.com.

Heffernan, William, and Mary Hendrickson. "Concentration of Agricultural Markets." *National Farmer's Union.* April 2007. Accessed March 25, 2009. http://www.nfu.org.

Hegeman, Roxana. "Injuries Propel Union's Offences." *Arkansas Democrat Gazette.* February 18, 2007. Accessed March 27, 2009. http://www. nwanews.com.

Herman, Judith. *Trauma and Recovery: The Aftermath of Violence—From Domestic Abuse to Political Terror.* New York: Basic Books, 1997.

Hindley, M. Patricia. "'Minding Animals': The Role of Animals in Children's Mental Development." In *Attitudes to Animals: Views in Animal Welfare,* edited by F. L. Dolins, 186–99. Cambridge, UK: Cambridge University Press, 1999.

Holm, Lotte, and M. Mohl. "The Role of Meat in Everyday Food Culture: An Analysis of an Interview Study in Copenhagen." *Appetite* 34 (2000): 277–83.

Howard, George S. *Ecological Psychology: Creating a More Earth-Friendly Human Nature.* Notre Dame, IN: University of Notre Dame Press, 1997.

Human Rights Watch. "Blood, Sweat and Fear." HRW.org. January 24, 2005. Accessed March 4, 2020. http://www.hrw.org.

Humane Society of the United States. "Undercover Investigation Reveals Rampant Animal Cruelty at California Slaughter Plant—A Major Beef Supplier to America's School Lunch Program." January 2008. Accessed March 26, 2009. http://www.hsus.org.

Irvin, David. "Control Debate, Growers Advised." *Arkansas-Democrat Gazette,* Northwest Arkansas edition. September 22, 2007. Accessed March 26, 2009. http://www.nwanews.com.

Jabs, Jennifer, Carol Devine, and J. Sobal. "Model of the Process of Adopting Vegetarian Diets: Health Vegetarians and Ethical Vegetarians." *Journal of Nutrition Education* 30, no. 4 (1998): 196–202.

Jacobsen, Ken, and Linda Riebel. *Eating to Save the Earth: Food Choices for a Healthy Planet.* Berkeley, CA: Celestial Arts, 2002.

Johns Hopkins Bloomberg School of Public Health. "Public Health Association Calls for Moratorium on Factory Farms; Cites Health Issues, Pollution." January 9, 2004. Accessed March 4, 2020. http:// www.jhsph.edu.

Johnson, Allan G. *The Forest and the Trees: Sociology as Life, Practice and Promise.* Philadelphia: Temple University Press, 1997.

Joy, Melanie. "From Carnivore to Carnist: Liberating the Language of Meat." *Satya* 8, no. 2 (2001): 26–27.

————. "Humanistic Psychology and Animal Rights: Reconsidering the Boundaries of the Humanistic Ethic." *Journal of Humanistic Psychology* 45, no. 1 (2005): 106–30.

————. "Psychic Numbing and Meat Consumption: The Psychology of Carnism." Dissertation, Saybrook Graduate School, 2003.

————. *Strategic Action for Animals: A Handbook on Strategic Movement Building, Organizing, and Activism for Animal Liberation.* New York: Lantern Books, 2008.

Jung, C. G. "The Problem of Evil Today." In *Meeting the Shadow: The Hidden Power of the Dark Side of Human Nature,* edited by C. Zweig and J. Abrams, 170–73. New York: Putnam, 1991.

Kapleau, Philip. *To Cherish All Life: A Buddhist Case for Becoming Vegetarian.* Rochester, NY: The Zen Center, 1986.

Kellert, Stephen R., and Alan Felthous. "Childhood Cruelty toward Animals among Criminals and Noncriminals." *Human Relations* 38, no. 12 (1985): 1113–29.

Kelly, Daniel. "The Role of Psychology in the Study of Culture." Purdue University. Accessed March 4, 2020. http://web.ics.purdue.edu.

Kirby, Alex, "Fish Do Feel Pain, Scientists Say." *BBC News Online.* Accessed March 4, 2020. http://news.bbc.co.uk.

Kowalski, Gary. *The Souls of Animals.* Walpole, NH: Stillpoint, 1991.

Lea, Emma, and Anthony Worsley. "Influences on Meat Consumption in Australia." *Appetite* 36 (2001): 127–36.

Lee, Jennifer. "Neighbors of Vast Hog Farms Say Foul Air Endangers Their Health." *New York Times.* May 11, 2003. Accessed March 4, 2020. http://www.nytimes.com.

Lemonick, Michael. "Why We Get Disgusted." *Time.* May 24, 2007. Accessed March 26, 2009. http://www.time.com.

Lifton, Robert Jay. "Beyond Psychic Numbing: A Call to Awareness." *American Journal of Orthopsychiatry* 52, no. 4 (1982): 619–29.

————. *The Nazi Doctors: Medical Killing and the Psychology of Genocide.* New York: Basic Books, 1986.

————. "A Nuclear Age Ethos: Ten Psychological-Ethical Principles." *Journal of Humanistic Psychology* 25, no. 4 (1985): 39–40.

Lifton, Robert Jay, and Eric Markusen. *The Genocidal Mentality: Nazi Holocaust and Nuclear Threat.* New York: Basic Books, 1990.

Lilliston, Ben. "A Fair Farm Bill for Competitive Markets." Institute for Agriculture and Trade Policy. 2007. Accessed March 29, 2009. http://www.agobservatory.org.

Lindeman, Marjaana, and M. Väänänen. "Measurement of Ethical Food Choice Motives." *Appetite* 34 (2000): 55–59.

LJ. "Stop the Dog Meat Industry." ASPCA Online Community. February 18, 2009. Accessed March 26, 2009. Information had been removed from ASPCA's website by January 21, 2020.

Lobo, Phillip. "Animal Welfare and Activism: What You Need to Know." PowerPoint presentation at the FMI-AMI Meat Conference. March 10, 2008. Accessed March 4, 2020. http://www.meatconference.com.

Locatelli, Margaret Garrett, and Robert Holt. "Antinuclear Activism, Psychic Numbing, and Mental Health." *International Journal of Mental Health* 15, no. 1–3 (1986): 143–61.

Lovelock, James. *Gaia: A New Look at Life on Earth.* Oxford, UK: Oxford University Press, 1979.

Macy, Joanna. "Working through Environmental Despair." In *Ecopsychology: Restoring the Earth, Healing the Mind,* edited by T. Roszak, M. E. Gomes, and A. D. Kanner, 240–59. San Francisco: Sierra Club Books, 1995.

Marcus, Erik. *Meat Market: Animals, Ethics, and Money.* Ithaca, NY: Brio Press, 2005.

———. *Vegan: The New Ethics of Eating.* Ithaca, NY: McBooks, 1998.

Maslow, Abraham. *Motivation and Personality.* 3rd ed. New York: Harper & Row, 1987.

Masson, Jeffrey. *The Face on Your Plate: The Truth about Food.* New York: W.W. Norton, 2009.

Mattera, Philip. "USDA Inc.: How Agribusiness Has Hijacked Regulatory Policy at the U.S. Department of Agriculture." Corporate research project of Good Jobs First. July 23, 2004. Accessed March 25, 2009. http://www.agribusinessaccountability.org.

Mattes, Richard D. "Learned Food Aversions: A Family Study." *Physiology and Behavior* 50 (1991): 499–504.

Maurer, Donna. *Vegetarianism: Movement or Moment?* Philadelphia: Temple University Press, 2002.

McDonald, Barbara, Ronald M. Cervero, and Bradley C. Courtenay. "An Ecological Perspective of Power in Transformational Learning: A Case Study of Ethical Vegans." *Adult Education Quarterly* 50, no. 1 (1999): 5–23.

McDougall, John A., and Mary McDougall. *The McDougall Program: Twelve Days to Dynamic Health.* New York: Plume, 1991.

McElroy, Damien. "Korean Outrage as West Tries to Use World Cup to Ban Dog Eating." *Telegraph.* January 6, 2002. Accessed March 4, 2020. http://www.telegraph.co.uk.

Messina, Virginia, and Mark Messina. *The Vegetarian Way.* New York: Crown Trade Paperbacks, 1996.

Metzner, Ralph. *Green Psychology: Transforming Our Relationship to the Earth.* Rochester, VT: Park Street Press, 1999.

Midei, Aimee. "Identification of the First Gene in Posttraumatic Stress Disorder." *Bio-Medicine.* September 22, 2002. Accessed March 4, 2020. http://news.bio-medicine.org.

Midgley, Mary. *Animals and Why They Matter: A Journey Around the Species Barrier.* New York: Penguin, 1983.

Milgram, Stanley. *Obedience to Authority: An Experimental View.* New York: Harper & Row, 1974.

Mintz, Sidney. *Tasting Food, Tasting Freedom: Excursions into Eating, Culture, and the Past.* Boston: Beacon Press, 1996.

Mitchell, C. E. "Animals—Sacred or Secondary? Ideological Influences on Therapist and Client Priorities and Approaches to Decision-Making." *Psychology* 30, no. 1 (1993): 22–28.

Mittal, Anuradha. "Giving Away the Farm: The 2002 Farm Bill." The Oakland Institute. June 2002. Accessed March 27, 2009. http://www. oaklandinstitute.org. The Oakland Institute is a policy think tank whose focus is on increasing public participation in, and fair debate on, critical social and environmental issues. Anuradha Mittal (the institute's executive director) was named most valuable thinker of 2008 by *Nation* magazine.

"More Urban, Suburban Homes Have Pet Chickens." *Dallas Morning News.* July 16, 2007. Accessed March 27, 2009. http://www.dallasnews.com.

Morgan, Dan, Gilbert M. Gaul, and Sarah Cohen. "Harvesting Cash: A Year-Long Investigation into Farm Subsidies." *Washington Post.* 2006. Accessed March 4, 2020. http://www.washingtonpost.com.

Morrow, Julie. "An Overview of Current Dairy Welfare Concerns from the North American Perspective." December 19, 2002. Accessed March 4, 2020. http://www.nal.usda.gov.

Motovalli, Jim. "The Meat of the Matter: Our Livestock Industry Creates More Greenhouse Gas than Transportation Does." *E Magazine* 19.4 (July/Aug. 2008).

Murcott, A. "You Are What You Eat: Anthropological Factors Influencing Food Choice." In *The Food Consumer,* edited by Christopher Ritson, Leslie Gofton, and John McKenzie, 107–25. New York: John Wiley & Sons, 1986.

National Endowment for the Humanities. "Voting Rights for Women: Pro- and Anti- Suffrage." *EDSITEment.com.* June 11, 2002. Accessed March 27, 2009. http://edsitement.neh.gov.

National Resources Defense Council. "Pollution from Giant Livestock Farms Threatens Public Health." July 15, 2005. Accessed March 4, 2020. http://www.nrdc.org.

"Nebraska Beef Recalls 1.2 Million Pounds of Beef." *MSNBC.com.* August 10, 2008. Accessed March 27, 2009. http://www.msnbc.msn.com.

Nestle, Marion. *Food Politics: How the Food Industry Influences Nutrition and Health.* Berkeley: University of California Press, 2007.

Nibert, David Allen. *Animal Rights/Human Rights: Entanglements of Oppression and Liberation.* Lanham, MD: Rowman & Littlefield, 2002.

Norberg-Hodge, Helena. "Compassion in the Age of the Global Economy." *The Psychology of Awakening: Buddhism, Science, and Our Day-to-Day Lives,* edited by G. Watson, S. Batchelor, and G. Claxton, 55–67. York Beach, ME: Samuel Weiser, 2000.

Passariello, Phyllis. "Me and My Totem: Cross-Cultural Attitudes towards Animals." *Attitudes to Animals: Views in Animal Welfare,* edited by F. L. Dolins, 12–25. Cambridge, UK: Cambridge University Press, 1999.

Patterson, Charles. *Eternal Treblinka: Our Treatment of Animals and the Holocaust.* New York: Lantern Books, 2002.

Petrinovich, L., P. O'Neill, and M. Jorgensen. "An Empirical Study of Moral Intuition: Toward an Evolutionary Ethics." *Journal of Personality and Social Psychology* 64, no. 3 (1993): 467–78.

Phillips, Mary T. "Savages, Drunks, and Lab Animals: The Researcher's Perception of Pain." *Society and Animals* 1, no. 1 (1993): 61–81.

Phillips, R. L. "Coronary Heart Disease Mortality among Seventh Day Adventists with Differing Dietary Habits; a Preliminary Report." *Cancer Epidemiology, Biomarkers and Prevention* 13 (2004): 1665.

Physicians Committee for Responsible Medicine. "The Protein Myth." Accessed March 26, 2009. http://www.pcrm.org.

Pickert, Kate. "Undercover Animal-Rights Investigator" *Time.* March 9, 2009. Accessed March 26, 2009. http://www.time.com.

Pilisuk, Marc. "Cognitive Balance and Self-Relevant Attitudes." *Journal of Abnormal and Social Psychology* 6, no. 2 (1962): 95–103.

———. "The Hidden Structure of Contemporary Violence." *Peace and Conflict: Journal of Peace Psychology* 4 (1998): 197–216.

Pilisuk, Marc, and Melanie Joy. "Humanistic Psychology and Ecology." *The Handbook of Humanistic Psychology: Leading Edges in Theory, Research and Practice,* edited by K. J. Schneider, J.T. Bugental, and J. F. Pierson, 101–14. Thousand Oaks, CA: Sage Publications, 2000.

Plous, Scott. "Psychological Mechanisms in the Human Use of Animals." *Journal of Social Issues* 49, no. 1 (1993): 11–52.

Pollan, Michael. *The Omnivore's Dilemma: A Natural History of Four Meals.* New York: Penguin, 2006.

———. "Power Steer." *New York Times.* March 31, 2002, sec. 6.

Prilleltensky, Isaac. "Psychology and the Status Quo." *American Psychologist* 44, no. 5 (1989): 795–802.

Public Broadcasting Service (PBS). "Meatpacking in the U.S.: Still a 'Jungle' Out There?" Episode description for the news program *NOW.* December 15, 2006. Accessed March 4, 2020. http://www.pbs.org.

Ramachandran, V. S. "Mirror Neurons and the Brain in the Vat." *Edge: The Third Culture.* January 10, 2006. Accessed March 26, 2009. http://www.edge.org.

Randour, Mary Lou. *Animal Grace: Entering a Spiritual Relationship with Our Fellow Creatures.* Novato, CA: New World Library, 2000.

Regan, Tom. *The Case for Animal Rights.* Berkeley: University of California Press, 1983.

"Retailer Recalls Parkas Trimmed in Dog Fur." *New York Times.* December 16, 1998. Accessed March 4, 2020. http://www.nytimes.com.

Richardson, N. J. "UK Consumer Perceptions of Meat." *Proceedings of the Nutrition Society* 53 (1994): 281–87.

Richardson, N. J., R. Shepard, and N. A. Elliman. "Current Attitudes and Future Influences on Meat Consumption in the U.K." *Appetite* 21 (1993): 41–51.

Rifkin, Jeremy. *Beyond Beef: The Rise and Fall of the Cattle Culture.* New York: Plume, 1992.

Robbins, John. *Diet for a New America.* Tiburon, CA: H. J. Kramer, 1987.

———. *The Food Revolution: How Your Diet Can Help Save Your Life and the World.* Berkeley, CA: Conari Press, 2001.

Rogers, Carl. *On Becoming a Person.* Boston: Houghton Mifflin, 1961.

"Role of the Meat and Poultry Industry in the U.S. Economy." *American Meat Institute.* 2000. Accessed November 1, 2001. http://www.meatami.com.

Rosen, Steven. *Diet for Transcendence: Vegetarianism and the World Religions.* Badger, CA: Torchlight Publishing, 1997.

Rostler, Suzanne. "Vegetarian Diet May Mask Eating Disorder in Teens." *Journal of Adolescent Health* 29 (2001): 406–16.

Rozin, Paul. "Moralization." In *Morality and Health,* edited by A. Brandt and P. Rozin, 379–401. New York: Rutledge, 1997.

———. "A Perspective on Disgust." *Psychological Review* 94, no. 1 (1987): 23–41.

Rozin, Paul, and April Fallon. "The Psychological Categorization of Foods and Non-Foods: A Preliminary Taxonomy of Food Rejections." *Appetite* 1 (1980): 193–201.

Rozin, Paul, Maureen Markwith, and Caryn Stoess. "Moralization and Becoming a Vegetarian: The Transformation of Preferences into Values and the Recruitment of Disgust." *Psychological Science* 8, no. 2 (1977): 67–73.

Rozin, Paul, M. L. Pelchat, and A. E. Fallon. "Psychological Factors Influencing Food Choice." In *The Food Consumer,* edited by C. Ritson, L. Gofton, and J. McKenzie, 85–106. New York: John Wiley & Sons, 1986.

Ryder, Richard D. *The Political Animal: The Conquest of Speciesism.* Jefferson, NC: McFarland & Company, 1998.

Sapp, Stephen G., and Wendy J. Harrod. "Social Acceptability and Intentions to Eat Beef: An Expansion of the Fishbein-Ajzen Model Using Reference Group Theory." *Rural Sociology* 54, no. 3 (1989): 420–38.

Schafer, Robert, and Elizabeth A. Yetley. "Social Psychology of Food Faddism." *Journal of the American Dietetic Association* 66 (1975): 129–133.

Schlosser, Eric. "The Chain Never Stops." *Mother Jones.* July/August 2001. Accessed March 4, 2020. http://www.motherjones.com.

———. *Fast Food Nation: The Dark Side of the All-American Meal.* New York: Houghton Mifflin, 2001.

———. "Fast Food Nation: Meat and Potatoes." *Rolling Stone.* September 3, 1998. www.rollingstone.com.

———. "Tyson's Moral Anchor." *The Nation.* June 24, 2004. Accessed March 27, 2009. http://www.thenation.com.

Schnall, Simone, Jonathan Haidt, and Gerald L. Clore. "Disgust as Embodied Moral Judgment." *Personality and Social Psychology Bulletin* 34, no. 8 (2008): 1096–109.

Schwartz, Richard H. *Judaism and Vegetarianism.* New York: Lantern Books, 2001.

Scully, Matthew. *Dominion: The Power of Man, the Suffering of Animals, and the Call to Mercy.* New York: St. Martin's Griffin Press, 2002.

Serpell, James A. *In the Company of Animals.* New York: Basil Blackwell, 1986.

———. "Sheep in Wolves' Clothing? Attitudes to Animals among Farmers and Scientists." In *Attitudes to Animals: Views in Animal Welfare,* edited F. L. Dolins, 26–33. Cambridge, UK: Cambridge University Press, 1999.

Severson, Kim. "Upton Sinclair, Now Playing on You Tube." *New York Times.* March 12, 2008. Accessed March 4, 2020. http://www.nytimes.com.

Shapiro, Kenneth J. "Animal Rights Versus Humanism: The Charge of Speciesism." *Journal of Humanistic Psychology* 30, no. 2 (1990): 9–37.

Shepard, Paul. *The Tender Carnivore and the Sacred Game.* New York: Scribners, 1973.

Shickle, D., et al. "Differences in Health, Knowledge and Attitudes between Vegetarians and Meat Eaters in a Random Population Sample." *Journal of the Royal Society of Medicine* 82 (1989): 18–20.

"Short Supply of Inspectors Threatens Meat Safety." MSNBC.com. February 21, 2008. Accessed March 27, 2009. http://www.msnbc.msn.com.

Simoons, Frederick J. *Eat Not This Flesh: Food Avoidances in the Old World.* Madison: University of Wisconsin Press, 1961.

Sims, L. S. "Food-Related Value-Orientations, Attitudes, and Beliefs of Vegetarians and Non-Vegetarians." *Ecology of Food and Nutrition* 7 (1978): 23–35.

Sinclair, Upton. *The Jungle.* New York: Penguin Classics, 2006.

Singer, Peter. *Animal Liberation.* New York: Avon Books, 1990.

Slovic, Paul. "'If I Look at the Mass I Will Never Act': Psychic Numbing and Genocide." *Judgment and Decision Making* 2, no. 2 (2007): 79–95.

Smith, Allen C., and Sherryl Kleinman. "Managing Emotions in Medical School: Students' Contacts with the Living and the Dead." *Social Psychology Quarterly* 52, no. 1 (1989): 56–69.

Sneddon, L. U., V. A. Braithwaite, and M. J. Gentle. "Do Fishes Have Nociceptors? Evidence for the Evolution of a Vertebrate Sensory System." *Proceedings of the Royal Society of London*, B 270. 1520 (June 7, 2003): 1115–21.

Spencer, Colin. *The Heretic's Feast: A History of Vegetarianism.* Hanover, NH: University Press of New England, 1995.

Spiegel, Marjorie. *The Dreaded Comparison: Human and Animal Slavery.* New York: Mirror Books, 1988.

Stamm, B. Hudnall, ed. *Secondary Traumatic Stress: Self-Care Issues for Clinicians, Researchers, and Educators.* 2nd ed. Baltimore, MD: Sidran Press, 1999.

Stepaniak, Joanne. *The Vegan Sourcebook.* Los Angeles: Lowell House, 1998.

Stout, Martha. *The Sociopath Next Door.* New York: Broadway Books, 2005.

Thich Nhat Hanh. *For a Future to Be Possible: Commentaries on the Five Wonderful Precepts.* Berkeley, CA: Parallax Press, 1993.

Tolle, Eckhart. *A New Earth: Awakening to Your Life's Purpose.* New York: Plume, 2005.

———. *The Power of Now: A Guide to Spiritual Enlightenment.* Novato, CA: New World Library, 1999.

Tsouderos, Trine. "Some Facial Expressions Are Part of a Primal 'Disgust Response', University of Toronto Study Finds." *Chicago Tribune.* February 27, 2009. Accessed March 26, 2009. http://www.chicagotribune.com.

Twigg, Julia. "Vegetarianism and the Meanings of Meat." In *The Sociology of Food and Eating,* edited by A. Murcott, and A. Aldershot, 18–30. England: Gomer Publishing, 1983.

Union of Concerned Scientists. "Outbreak of a Resistant Food Borne Illness." July 18, 2003. Accessed March 27, 2009. http://www.ucsusa.org.

———. "They Eat What? The Reality of Feed at Animal Factories." August 8, 2006. Accessed March 27, 2009. http://www.ucsusa.org.

US Department of Agriculture. "Nebraska Firm Recalls Beef Products Due to Possible E. coli O157:H7 Contamination." June 30, 2008. Accessed March 27, 2009. http://www.fsis.usda.gov.

US Department of Agriculture, Grain Inspection, Packers, and Stockyards Administration (GIPSA). Accessed March 30, 2009. http://www.gipsa.usda.gov. Statement of David R. Shipman, acting administrator of the Grain Inspection, Packers, and Stockyards Administration, before the Subcommittee on Agriculture, Rural Development, and Related Agencies, in reference to the FY 2003 budget proposal.

US Department of Labor. "Safety and Health Guide for the Meatpacking Industry." 1988. Accessed March 4, 2020. http://www.osha.gov.

Vann, Madeline. "High Meat Consumption Linked to Heightened Cancer Risk." *U.S. News and World Report.* December 11, 2007. Accessed March 27, 2009. http://health.usnews.comusnews.

Vansickle, Joe. "Preparing Pigs for Transport." *The National Hog Farmer.* September 15, 2008. Accessed March 4, 2020. http://nationalhog farmer.com.

Verhovek, Sam. "Gain for Winfrey in Suit by Beef Producers in Texas." *New York Times.* February 18, 1998. Accessed March 27, 2009. http://query.nytimes.com.

Warrick, Joby. "They Die Piece by Piece." *Washington Post.* April 10, 2001. Accessed March 26, 2009. http://www.hfa.org.

Weingarten, Kaethe. *Common Shock: Witnessing Violence Every Day.* New York: New American Library, 2004.

WGBH Educational Foundation. "Inside the Slaughterhouse." Accessed March 4, 2020. http://www.pbs.org.

———. "What Is HAACP?" Accessed March 27, 2009. http://www.pbs.org.

Wheatley, Thalia, and Jonathon Haidt. "Hypnotically Induced Disgust Makes Moral Judgments More Severe." *Psychological Science* 16 (2005): 780–84.

Wolf, David B. "Social Work and Speciesism." *Social Work* 45, no. 1 (2000): 88–93.

Worldwatch Institute. "Worldwatch Institute: Vision for a Sustainable World." March 26, 2009. Accessed March 27, 2009. http://www.worldwatch.org.

Worsley, Anthony, and Grace Skrzypiec. "Teenage Vegetarianism Prevalence, Social and Cognitive Contexts." *Appetite* 30 (1998): 151–70.

Zey, Mary, and William Alex McIntosh. "Predicting Intent to Consume Beef: Normative Versus Attitudinal Influences." *Rural Sociology* 57, no. 2 (1992): 250–65.

Zur, Ofer. "On Nuclear Attitudes and Psychic Numbing: Overview and Critique." *Contemporary Social Psychology* 14, no. 2 (1990): 96–119.

Zwerdling, Daniel. "A View to a Kill." *Gourmet.* June 2007. Accessed March 26, 2009. http://www.gourmet.com.

Index

A

C

D

E

ecocarnism, 143–144
E. coli, 67, 68, 81
edible vs. inedible classifications,
    4–5, 112–113, 119–120
egg production, 47–48
Einstein, Albert, 85
Eisnitz, Gail, 33, 35, 40, 52, 72–74
electrocution, 56
emasculatome, 39
Emily the Sacred Cow, 125–127
emotional eating, 119–120
emotional reactions to foods, 2
empathy, 8–9, 115–117
    apathy to, 130–132

bear witness and, 128
biological basis for, 130
entrenched ideologies, 20, 21
environmental issues, carnism and,
    75–77, 134–135
Environmental Quality Incentives
    Program (EQIP), 80
erosion, 75, 135
escargots, 120
Eta, 75
ethics, 10–11, 17–18
European Union carnistic
    consumption, 25–26, 64–65

F

factory farms, 27
    cattle conditions, 38–41,
        50–51
    environmental issues caused
        by, 64, 75–76
    fish and sea life, 56–57
    pig, 30–36
    poultry, 42–45
farm-raised fish, 56
Fast Food Nation (Schlosser), 29, 65
fecal matter, 65, 67
feminism, 19–20
Fiddes, Nick, 69

fish, 53–57
    intelligence research on, 53–54
    legislation protecting, 54
    pain and, 54–55
    slaughter of, 55–57
    fishing, 55–56
Food and Water Watch, 68
food chain, 99, 133
food libel laws, 81
free choice, 96
Free Will, Myth of, 103–104
fresh water depletion, 75
fungicides, 65, 135

G

Game Changers, The (film), 135
Gandhi, Mahatma, 127
generalizations, schemas and, 4
gestation crates, 36, 88
Getting Relationships Right: How to Build
    Resilience and Thrive in Life, Love,
    and Work (Joy), 148
goats, 37, 63
goldfish, 54
Gourmet (magazine), 29

Grain Inspection, Packers and
    Stockyards Administration
    (GIPSA), 79
greenhouse gas emissions, 75
growth hormones, 50, 56, 64–65,
    135
Guanches of Canary Islands,
    butchers of, 75
Guardian, the, 67

H

I

J

Japan, butchers in, 75
JBS USA, 80
Jews, naturalized behaviors and, 98
Journal of Food Protection, 67
Joy, Sebastian, 142
Jungle, The (Sinclair), 65–66

justification, 9
    natural of, 87, 97–99
    necessary of, 87, 100–103
    normal of, 87, 96–97
    Three Ns of, described, 86–87

K

Kaplan, Helmut, 125
killing
    as economic imperative, 103
    human aversion to, 23–24

knowing without knowing
    phenomenon, 61
Korea Association for Animal
    Protection, 59
Korean dogmeat trade, 58–60

L

Lama, Eddie, 133
lameness, 50
LA Times, 49
legal person, 93–94
legal property, 93–94
legal system, 93
legitimization, 93–96

Lifton, Robert Jay, 77, 131
literal invisibility, 84
Little, Ellen, 126
live chilling, 56
lobbyists, 80
lobsters, 46–47, 54

M

mad cow disease, 81
mainstream, 20
Mandela, Nelson, 141
Marine Biological Laboratory, 54
Marshall, S. L. A., 23–24
mastitis, 50
The Matrix (film), 105–106
McCartney, Paul, 61
McDonalds, 88
McKown, Delos B., 12
meat
    perceptions of, 3–4
    perceptual process, 5
meat eater, 18, 53
Meat Inspection Act, 66

meatocracy, 81
meatpacking plants. *See also*
    slaughterhouses
    accident reports, 70
    human health issues, 63–65,
        69–70
    inspections at, 66–68
    operational hazards in, 71–72
    Sinclair exposé on, 65–66
    workers in, 64
Meat Trades Journal, 37
Milgram, Stanley, 90–92
milk production, 50
Mississippi State University, 36
Moby, 136

Moore, Dale, 79
moral emotion, 117
Moreno, Ramon, 41–42
Morris, Craig, 79–80
Moseley, James, 79
Mother Jones (magazine), 69

Mother Teresa, 111
mypetchicken.com, 42
mythmakers, 87–90
Myth of Free Will, 103–104
myth of necessity, 102–103
mythology of meat, 86–90

N

Nambikwara Indians of Brazil, 120
National Cattlemen's Beef
    Association (NCBA), 37, 79
National Dairy Council, 89–90
National Hog Farmer, The, 33
National Institutes of Health, 82
National Pork Board, 80
naturalization, 98–99
natural of justification, 87, 97–99
Nazi Doctors, The (Lifton), 131
necessary of justification, 87,
    100–103

neocarnism, 142–145
Nestor, Felicia, 68
Newcastle disease, 49
news media, 93, 94
Nin, Anais, 1
nonrelational systems, 147
normal of justification, 87, 96–97
Norwegian School of Veterinary
    Science, 55
numbers, numbing and, 111
nutritionists, 89

O

obedience to authority study, 90–92
objectification defense, 9, 107–108
objectifying language, 107–108
Occupational Safety and Health
    Administration (OSHA), 70
O'Dea, James, 139
omission, 94
omnivore, 19

Omnivore's Dilemma, The (Pollan),
    37–38
Ontario Ministry of Agriculture,
    Food and Rural Affairs, 32
oppressive system, 22. *See also* violent
    ideology
Oxford University, 53–54

P

pain, animals and, 22–23
patriarchy, 20–21
Peace Abbey, 126, 127
Pearl, Bill, 136
Pennsylvania State University, 30
People for the Ethical Treatment of
    Animals (PETA), 74, 95
perceptions, 2. *See also* Cognitive Trio
    of animals/animal food, 2–6

    empathy to apathy, 8–9
    missing link in, process, 7–8
    schema and, 4
    shift in, 2–3
percussive stunning, 56
Perdue chicken slaughter plant, 44
person, legal, 93–94
pesticides, 56, 65, 77, 78
pig confinement buildings, 32–33

Q

R

S

T

U

About the Author

Dr. Melanie Joy is a Harvard-educated psychologist, celebrated speaker, and the author of five books, including the award-winning *Beyond Beliefs: A Guide to Improving Relationships and Communication for Vegans, Vegetarians, and Meat Eaters; Powerarchy: Understanding the Psychology of Oppression for Social Transformation;* and *Getting Relationships Right.* Her work has been featured in major media outlets around the world, and she has received a number of awards, including the Ahimsa Award—previously given to the Dalai Lama and Nelson Mandela—for her work on global nonviolence. Joy has given talks and trainings in over fifty countries, and she is also the founding president of the charitable organization Beyond Carnism. You can learn more about her work at *carnism.org.*